CONTENTS

FEATURED TITLES

BOB VAN LAERHOVEN   WILLIAM LUVAAS   BEN STOLTZFUS

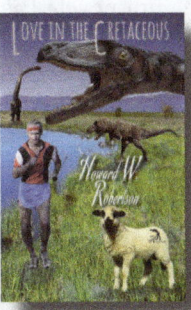

HOWARD W. ROBERTSON   WILLIAM J. PALMER   ANNA FAKTOROVICH

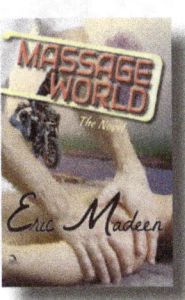
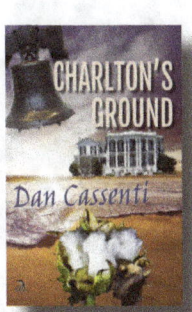
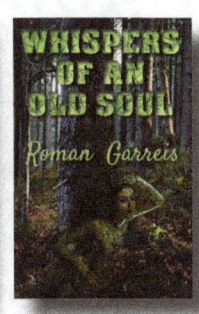

ERIC MADEEN   DAN CASSENTI   ROMAN GARREIS

NEW RELEASES

Two Cities ($15: $20, 256pp, 6X9": Softcover: ISBN-13: 978-1-68114-364-4; $35: Hardcover: ISBN-13: 978-1-68114-365-1; $2.99: EBook: ISBN-13: 978-1-68114-366-8; LCCN: 2017946908; Ecological Thriller; Release: November 1, 2017; Nominated for the 2017 Pushcart Prize): A bi-coastal political eco-thriller, it is set in Washington D.C. and Los Angeles in the near present. Played out against the backdrop of a dysfunctional government and the lobbying power of Big Oil, two brothers, one a Washington political activist, the other a Los Angeles celebrity lawyer, fall under the spell of a charismatic eco-rock singer and activist who is organizing the biggest protest march in history. When that march careens out of control and into tragedy, the brothers must deal with a kidnapping, a daring rescue attempt, and an inspired act of brotherly heroism right out of the Dickensian precursor that this novel channels.

WILLIAM J. PALMER is Professor Emeritus of English at Purdue University. The Uses of Money is his eighth novel. The four novels in his "Mr. Dickens" series of Victorian murder mysteries have been chosen as selections by numerous national book clubs, and have been translated into Spanish and Japanese. The three novels of his The Wabash Trilogy include a sports novel, a crime novel and a comic novel, all set in the Wabash valley of Indiana in the late 20th-Century. Website: wjpalmernovelist.wordpress.com

"The cities in William J. Palmer's new thriller Two Cities are Los Angeles and Washington, D.C., not London and Paris, and the conflict is not the French Revolution but a battle between the government and oil lobbyists and a powerful lobby called OceanSave that wants to prevent drilling in the Pacific." —*Akron Beacon Journal*, Lynne Sherwin

"Palmer maintains the fast-paced, high-stakes plot his thrill-seeking readers adore… Although the plot may be a work of fiction, the descriptions of Haitian life are very much based in reality. As research for the novel, Palmer interviewed several individuals who traveled to Haiti on mission trips." —*Purdue Exponent*, Alyssa Fanara, "Author addresses Haitian living conditions, corruption in new thriller novel," October 12, 2016

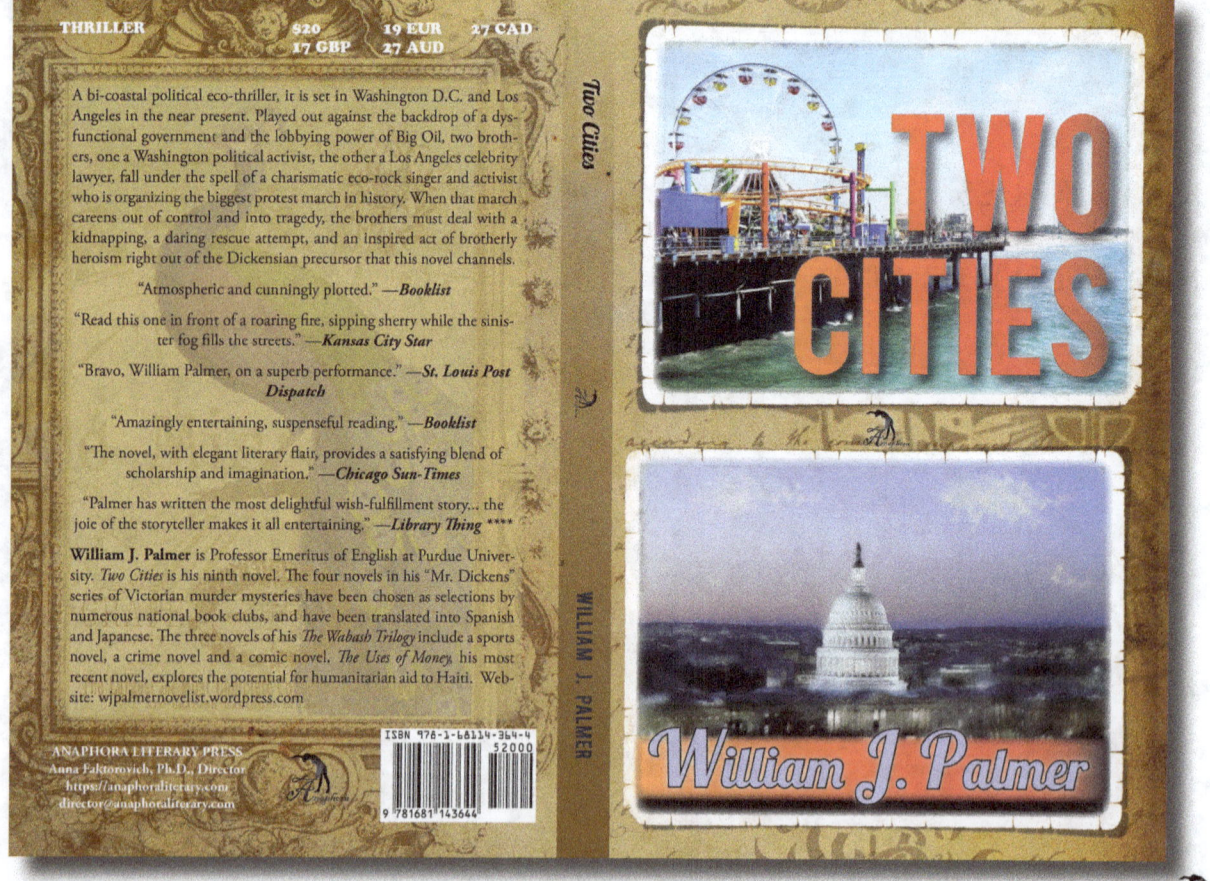

The Last Mermaid Princess ($20, 220pp, 6X9": Softcover: ISBN: 978-1-68114-433-7; $35: Hardcover: ISBN: 978-1-68114-434-4; $2.99: Ebook: ISBN: 978-1-68114-435-1; LCCN: 2018947710; Fiction—Women; Edited by: Alicia S. Jacques; Release: November 19, 2018): Lily Chaidee was never at home with herself, her family, or her geography, and as a hybrid-Asian growing up in the Texas Panhandle during the 1960's, she was ill-equipped to face the challenges that would inevitably come. Amarillo, an inhospitable place for an ethnically diverse family, was only part of the problem. Mental illness, sexual predation, addiction, and hypocrisy lay formidable difficulties in her path. But Lily was smart, and smart people often find ways to triumph over horrific circumstances. Even if she could claim her joy, sometimes the worst enemy dwells within. Lily must seek her peace and her place in order to rise above the things that bind her.

LILY LEWIS is a warrior in the battle against ignorance and injustice both in the classroom and in the community. where she is active in catalyzing positive change. Three extraordinary children and four grandchildren illuminate her path and comprise her universe. Although she loves to travel, her place of wonder will always be the deep blue sea. She is a survivor, living one day at a time, with her life partner and two cats, Sophie and Sylvester.

"The author, Lily Lewis, writes beautifully, full of emotion even when she recounts the darkest times. She has a wonderful command of the written word, with descriptive phrases that resonate with the reader... I found the whole book to be a compelling read, and I know it will be a story that will stay with me for a long time. Such was the skill of writing that I felt a personal attachment to Lily, even empathizing when she made blatant mistakes and acted inappropriately, or made decisions that would clearly end in disaster... I have rarely felt such strong feelings for an author, and I commend Lily Lewis for conveying every conceivable emotion with exquisite prose in a gripping and heart-wrenching story." — Jewel Hart, Manager-Book Reviews & Marketing/Social Media Expert, *Chick Lit Cafe*

Book Trailer: https://youtu.be/3xn14P3UqLw

Falling and Other Stories (Softcover: $20, 122pp, 6X9": ISBN: 978-1-68114-454-2; Hardcover: $35: ISBN: 978-1-68114-455-9; EBook: $2.99: ISBN: 978-1-68114-456-6; LCCN: 2018907591; Fiction—Short Stories (single author); Edited by: Claire Adler; Release: October 1, 2018): a novella and six short fictions, is by turn mythic and realistic, moving and wistful, innovative and traditional. It maps a wide geography of human emotions: lust, adventure, love, alienation, explicit violence and implicit passion. Ben Stoltzfus makes each character—a glamour girl, a scuba queen, a shaman, a mountain climber, a skier, a ball-court superstar, women in distress, even strangers—come vividly alive. In "Falling" you, the narrator, climb toward the summit with Juan, your friend, following flashbacks in the narrative trail. In "The Bank", a father and son come to terms with a lifetime of estrangement. In "Glamour Girl", a woman reminisces about her husbands, rich people, Joe Louis and happy days in the spotlight. In "Scuba Queen", two college friends, now in their thirties, dive for abalone in the kelp beds of the Pacific Ocean where their rivalry begets a dangerous and miraculous denoument. "Masks and Bergamasks" is a love monologue, a silent conversation between a teacher and a student during a lecture on French Symbolist poetry. In "Samantha's Choice", three friends debate free will versus determinism, and are caught in an avalanche while skiing Mount Washington. In "The Games of Chichén Itzà", a shaman dreams Mayan life and ritual into a dramatic ball-court encounter between two teams; the play of the gods is re-enacted as struggle, blood-sacrifice and renewal. Subtly honed with hallmark precision and keen insight this wide-ranging collection exemplifies the best in narrative art.

BEN STOLTZFUS is Professor Emeritus of Comparative Literature and Creative Writing at the University of California, Riverside. He is a novelist, translator, literary critic and internationally recognized inter-arts scholar. He has published 12 monographs of literary criticism, five novels and one collection of short stories. *Romoland*, a pictonovel, his most recent publication, was written in collaboration with Judith Palmer, the artist. He has received many awards: Fulbright, Camargo, Gradiva, Humanities, Creative Arts, and MLA. Stoltzfus lives in Riverside, California, with Judith Palmer, his wife.

"The Eye of the Needle, a tour de force of the French form." —Richard Rhodes, *New York Times Book Review*

"As a work of art, this novel is superior!" —*London Telegraph*

Welcome to Saint Angel: ($20, 220pp, 6X9": Soft-cover ISBN: 978-1-68114-320-0; $35: Hardcover ISBN-13: 978-1-68114-321-7; $2.99: EBook ISBN: 978-1-68114-322-4; LCCN: 2017937186; Satire; Release: March 16, 2018): Iconoclastic inventor Al Sharpe loves his canyon home in Southern California's Saint Angel Valley. He builds his teenage daughter a tree house in a giant oak and invents the Sharpe Smoke Scrubber to detoxify wood smoke. When wealthy developer Ches Noonan, a fellow member of the Desert Green Lawn Association, sets out to fill the valley with houses and appropriate its precious water supply to fill swimming pools during California's worst drought, Al and his quixotic pals rebel. In the Realty Revenge, they halt development through madcap high jinks and the help of local Indians, ancient demon Tahquitz, and mother nature. Welcome to Saint Angel is a dead-serious comedy about development gone mad and townsfolk's attempts to protect their rural Arcadia from bulldozers and climate change deniers. Part environmental fiction, part social satire, it speaks to exurban sprawl and the heedless development of fragile natural areas and to the power of communal resistance in the face of calamity.

WILLIAM LUVAAS has published three novels, *The Seductions of Natalie Bach, Going Under,* and *Beneath The Coyote Hills,* and two story collections, *A Working Man's Apocrypha* and *Ashes Rain Down: A Story Cycle, The Huffington Post's* 2013 Book of the Year and a finalist for the Next Generation Indie Book Awards. His honors include a National Endowment for the Arts Fellowship, first place in Glimmer Train's Fiction Open Contest, The Ledge Magazine's Fiction Contest, and Fiction Network's 2nd National Fiction Competition. His work has appeared in dozens of publications, including *Antioch Review, The American Fiction Anthology, Glimmer Train, Grain Mag., North American Review, The Sun, Texas Review, The Village Voice* and *The Washington Post Book World.* He has taught writing at San Diego State University, U.C. Riverside, and The Writers Voice in New York, and is Online Fiction Editor for *Cutthroat: A Journal of the Arts.* Luvaas lives in Los Angeles with his wife Lucinda, an artist and film maker.

Book Trailer: Won **Best Adapted Screenplay Award** at the Golden State Film Festival: https://vimeo.com/266250466

"All wounds are ripe for reopening in this sure-fire satire of contemporary America: social divisions and bitter personal animosities; wealth, possessions and power versus the assertion of individual rights; arrogant, rapacious humankind versus vulnerable nature....Fortunately for the reader, this author's passion–his anger, too–come wrapped in a healthy sense of the absurd....And the reader is caught, along with Luvaas, in a parlous place somewhere between outrage and hilarity." —*Los Angeles Review of Books*, Peter Clothier, "Between Outrage and Hilarity: William Luuvas's Welcome to Saint Angel", April 12, 2018

"Welcome to Saint Angel is a love story. It's about a love of the land, a love of place, a love of community, a love of humanity, flawed and full of missteps and mistakes as it may be. It's about a love that connects people and places." —Elan Barnehama, **Forth Magazine**

"William Luvaas writes with immense verve and imagination, and has a gift for humour." —Jack Messenger, **Feed the Monkey**

Love in the Cretaceous ($20, 130pp, 6X9": Softcover ISBN-13: 978-1-68114-332-3; $35: Hardcover ISBN: 978-1-68114-333-0; $2.99: EBook ISBN-13: 978-1-68114-334-7; LCCN: 2017905568; Literary Fiction: Genetic Engineering; October 15, 2017): takes place in a dinosaur park in Oregon a hundred years in the future. Ted Beebe has lost the love of his life and must suddenly find his way alone in old age. He finds young people to take the place of his wife and himself in assuring the survival of Cretaceous World, the park his wife and he created. Global warming has proceeded as predicted, and the fate of *Homo sapiens* has become obviously uncertain. People come to see the genetically engineered recreations of dinosaurs and are made more aware of humanity's own vulnerability to extinction. Ted succeeds in creating a new family structure whose three generations will guide the park through the immediate future. He also keeps alive his wife's memory while coping with the challenges of the uncertain future.

HOWARD W. ROBERTSON lives in Eugene, Oregon, where his ancestors arrived as members of the Lost Wagon Train of 1853. He has previously published two books of fiction and ten books of poetry. He has won the Sinclair Poetry Prize, the Robinson Jeffers Prize for Poetry, the Bumbershoot Award, and numerous other competitions. His work has been published in *Nest, Literal Latté, Nimrod, Fireweed,* and many other journals. His poetry has been anthologized in many collections, including *The Clear Cut Future* and *The Ahsahta Anthology: Poetry of the American West.* His work has been deeply influenced by a lifelong love of Russian literature. For more about Howard W. Robertson, see his webpage: www.howardwrobertson.com.

"Rollicking, fresh, engaging, offbeat, zany, memorable." —***Publishers Weekly***

"Turns everything you learned from Jurassic Park on its head. The thrills in this one are metaphysical as well as primordial." —*SeattleReviewofBooks.com*

"The descriptions of Cretaceous World and its formidable inhabitants are vivid and realistic and Robertson displays a wry sense of humor and a panoply of intriguing characters. Most of the action takes place in the theme park and Robertson draws several thought-provoking parallels between the dinosaurs and their human caretakers… Robertson's playful and keen sense of humor is another highlight, particularly the teasing banter between Lana and Ted and a popular local restaurant whimsically named Hominid's Delight." —*Kirkus Review*, November 14, 2017

The Map is not the Territory ($15, 86pp, 6X9"): Paperback: ISBN: 978-1-68114-415-3; $30: Hardcover: ISBN: 978-1-68114-416-0; $2.99: EBook: ISBN: 978-1-68114-417-7; LCCN: 2018900255; Poetry—Subjects & Themes—Nature; Release: April 15, 2018): The poems explore states of consciousness triggered by the author's connections to the land where he resides in Central Vermont and the cityscapes that he is intimate with in Brooklyn, New York. They are also informed by his long-time practices of zazen meditation and t'ai chi and his ongoing study of western and eastern philosophy and psychology.

PETER SCHNEIDER is a poet and psychotherapist who lives in Brooklyn, NY and Rochester, VT. His poems have appeared or are forthcoming in *AMP: The Journal of Digital Literature* (Hofstra University); *The Buddhist Poetry Review; Mobius: The Journal of Social Change; The Shot-glass Journal; Kairos*; and in the broadside collection, *A Midnight Snack*. His MFA is from Columbia University School of the Arts and his PhD is in clinical psychology from New York University.

"Awake and in love with the natural world, these poems merge psychological and spiritual landscapes with rivers, trees, and seasons in vital ways. Schneider's poems are rooted and moving, lingering in and traveling through American towns, flowers, human bodies, and philosophies. With exactitude and vastness, the poems speak to the beautiful strangeness of ordinary things while keeping a sly grin: 'Refuge is swaying / side to side leaning over / on one's black cushion / to cut a loud fart.' We need these grounded, funny, wise and open poems in the world. They show us the vibrancy of a 'gray winter morning' for the first time all over again." —Maya Pindyck, *Emoticoncert* (Four Way Books) and *Friend Among Stones* (New Rivers Press)

Book Trailer: https://youtu.be/pS-Ens_TRjY

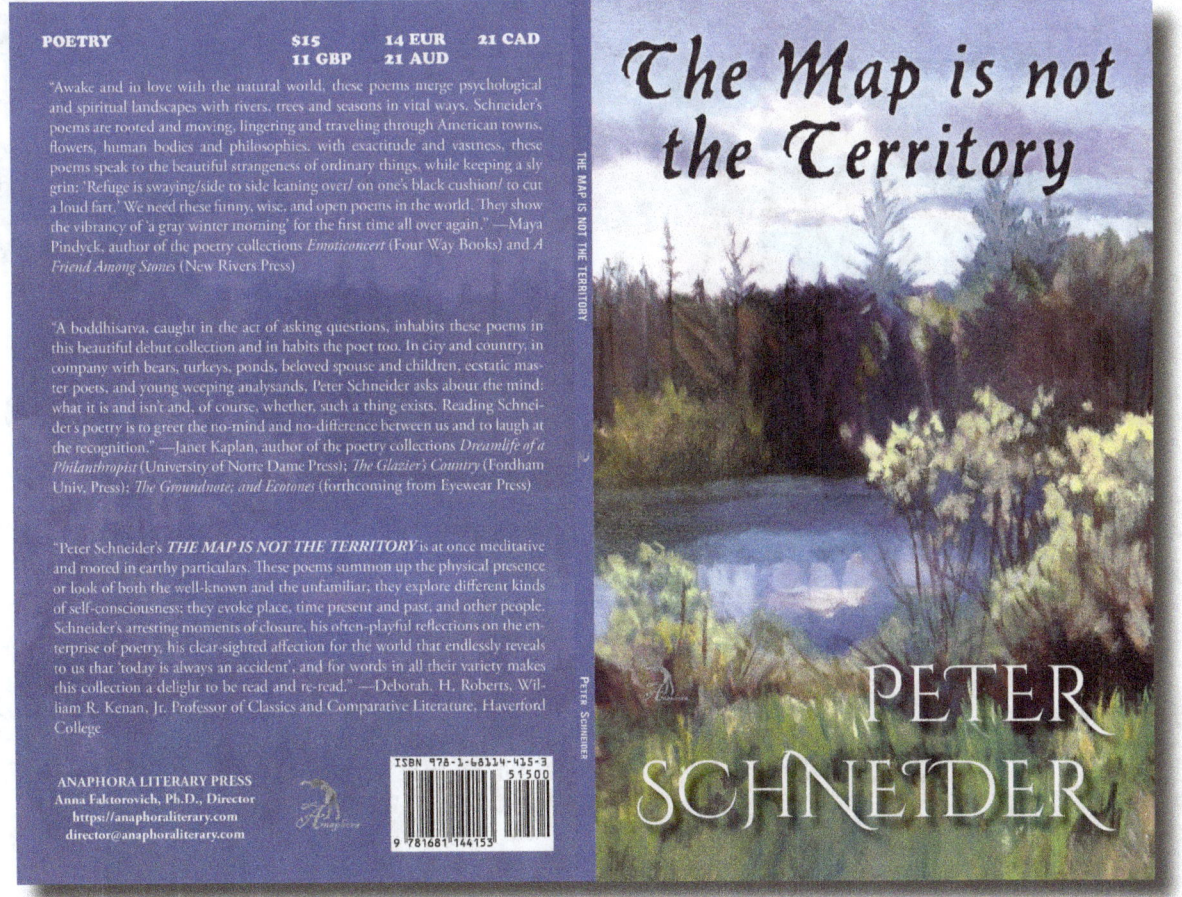

The Burden of Persuasion ($20: Softcover ISBN-13: 978-1-68114-323-1; $35: Hardcover ISBN-13: 978-1-68114-324-8; $2.99: EBook ISBN-13: 978-1-68114-325-5; LCCN: 2017937187; Mystery; Release: October 16, 2017): The trauma of retiring early forces FBI Special Agent B. Clare Ryan to conduct an unsanctioned investigation into one of her first cases for the Bureau back in 1988. After an unfavorable verdict that was the culmination of eight years of litigation over claims of sexual harassment of Ida Callaghan by the management at the Bedford Bank in Manhattan, her father, Bradley, shot the judge over the case, Vincente Brunetti, to death at his suburban residence before committing suicide. The case is outrageous enough on its own, but Ryan is more interested in why her supervisor at the FBI forbade her from investigating it and destroyed the suicide note that Bradley left behind. This clue leads her to a diary that accuses many powerful men in New York of corruption. Now in 2013, the trail might be cold, but Ryan digs up ancient records and does everything possible, including breaking into private vaults and morgues to get to the truth, which turns out to be more explosive than she predicted. Ryan reproduces original diaries, notes, letters, police reports and other documents that finally sufficiently prove the case that both Bradley and his daughter lost.

ANNA FAKTOROVICH is the Director and Founder of the Anaphora Literary Press. She taught college English for four years. She has a PhD in English Literature. She published two scholarly books: *Rebellion as Genre in the Novels of Scott, Dickens and Stevenson* (McFarland, 2013) and *The Formulas of Popular Fiction* (McFarland, 2014). She also published *Improvisational Arguments* (Fomite Press, 2011) and *The Great Love of Queen Margaret, the Vampire and Campaigns Against the Olden* (Grim's Labyrinth Publishing). She won the MLA Bibliography, Kentucky Historical Society and the Brown University research fellowships.

Heart Fever (Softcover: $15, 114pp, 6X9": ISBN: 978-1-68114-391-0; Hardcover: $30: ISBN: 978-1-68114-392-7; EBook: $2.99: ISBN: 978-1-68114-393-4; LCCN: 2017914844; Fiction—Mystery & Detective—Short Stories; Release: January 5, 2018): After his much-acclaimed short story collection *Dangerous Obsessions*, which had war as a common background, Belgian/Flemish author Van Laerhoven surprises again with five stories that shed piercing light on our most self-destructive impulses. A steroid-spiked Syrian mercenary of Bashar-al-Assad is determined to become a "martyr," after the loss of his right arm by "friendly fire." A retired London tube-driver becomes obsessed by his desire to revenge the vicious killing of his parents in Croatia on his half-nephew. A Belgian travel-writer gets entangled in the madness of the Kosovo-war during the nineties and witnesses its dramatic consequences many years later in New York. A jaded *art brut* painter in Brussels betrays his best friend, a Rwandese art forger, to the Mafia, opening the door to guilt, lust, and murder. A born liar with the nickname Johnny di Machio seeks in the seventies, in Poona, India, salvation in Bhagwan's ashram for his sexual problems, but gets trapped in a maze of long hidden violence.

Book Trailer: https://youtu.be/LRf6ujQPJB8

BOB VAN LAERHOVEN a fulltime Belgian/Flemish author, Laerhoven published more than 30 books in Holland and Belgium. Some of his literary work is also published in the US, Canada and France. Three times finalist of the Hercule Poirot Prize for best mystery novel of the year with the novels *Djinn* and *The Finger of God*. Winner of the Hercule Poirot Prize for *Baudelaire's Revenge*, which also won the USA Best Book Award 2014 in the category "mystery/suspense". His latest novel is *De schaduw van de Mol* (*The Shadow of the Mole*).

Rounding Third and Headed for Home ($15, 6X9", 106pp, 50 color drawings: Softcover ISBN: 978-1-68114-311-8; $30: Hardcover ISBN-13: 978-1-68114-312-5; $2.99: EBook ISBN-13: 978-1-68114-313-2; LCCN: 2017935586; Baseball Haikus; Edited by Nicholas Salvatore Pagano; Release: April 5, 2017): pays poetic tribute to fifty early stars and innovators of the game. Baseball is a game which links the generations and transcends the usual boundaries of time. The early pioneers believed that baseball revealed the physical strength, mental prowess, and inner fortitude and determination of the game's participants. As such, this book of poetry provides a glimpse into the lives of these baseball greats in a manner which celebrates their multifaceted, vibrant and unique lives both on and off the diamond.

DR. WILLIAM J. MALONEY is a clinical associate professor at New York University College of Dentistry. He is a fellow of the Academy of Dentistry International, the New York Academy of Medicine, the Royal Society of Medicine and the Pierre Fauchard Academy. Dr. Maloney is the author of over 270 professional publications. He has also been presented with the Award of Excellence from The Floating Hospital of New York City. He has also been inducted into various prestigious organizations and societies, such as The New York Academy of Medicine and The Royal Society of Medicine.

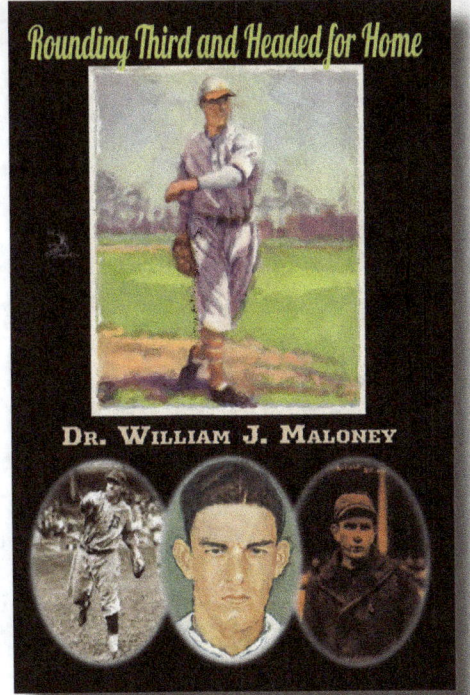

A CITIZEN'S GUIDE TO IMPROVING PUBLIC EDUCATION

SAVING K-12

What Happened to Our Public Schools? How Do We Fix Them?

BRUCE DEITRICK PRICE

Saving K-12: What Happened to Our Public Schools? How Do We Fix Them? ($20, 188pp, 6X9": Softcover: ISBN-13: 978-1-68114-361-3; $35: Hardcover: ISBN-13: 978-1-68114-362-0; $2.99: EBook: ISBN-13: 978-1-68114-363-7; LCCN: 2017946111; Educational Policy & Reform; Release: November 17, 2017): Public schools are a vast money pit. Education officials seem to prefer inefficiency and mediocrity. We could have better schools at less cost. This book explains how. Bruce Deitrick Price is the country's most prolific and aggressive writer on education. He is good at explaining the root causes, the problems that typically occur, and the ideological obsessions that lead our Education Establishment astray. This book presents 65 articles divided into 10 themes: Reading; Math; Weird Theories and Methods; Common Core; Historical Background; Guilty as Charged; Where Are Our Leaders; and What to Do Now. You can read the articles in any order and dip in wherever you want. This is pleasant reading about grim topics. If we don't save the public schools, we're not going to save very much else.

BRUCE DEITRICK PRICE is a novelist, artist, poet, and education reformer. He graduated with Honors in English Literature from Princeton and lived for many years in Manhattan where he ran a graphic design business. Along the way he was fascinated by the counterproductive practices so common in public schools. He founded Improve-Education.org in 2005.

"Bruce Price's Saving K-12 is a MUST read! It is precise, concise and powerful. Action is required… for the sake of our children, our grandchildren and the future of the American Republic!" —Robert W. Sweet, Jr., **President, The National Right to Read Foundation**

BIOGRAPHY

A Berkshire Boyhood ($20, ISBN: 978-1-937536-52-7, $35: Hardback ISBN: 978-1-68114-147-3, LCCN: 2013951941, 6X9", 162pp, April 2014): Neither celebrity-gawk, "misery memoir," nor confessional melodrama, *A Berkshire Boyhood* is more reminiscent of such memoirs as Tobias Wolff's *This Boy's Life* and Emily Fox Gordon's *Are You Happy? A Berkshire Boyhood* will strike readers as a parallel universe to Gordon's book, her own story of growing up in Williamstown, as a privileged faculty brat and young girl in the 1950s.

ROBERT J. BEGIEBING is the author of eight books, a play, and many articles and stories. His novel *Rebecca Wentworth's Distraction* won the Langum Prize for historical fiction. *The Strange Death of Mistress Coffin* was chosen as a Main Selection for the Mystery and Literary Guild Book Clubs and is currently optioned for a film. His most recent novel is *The Turner Erotica* (2013), about both the secret and public life and work of J.M.W. Turner. His fiction writing has been supported by grants from the Lila-Wallace Foundation and the New Hampshire Council for the Arts. In 2007, Governor John Lynch appointed Begiebing to the Council for the Arts. In 2009 he served as the inaugural faculty members at the Norman Mailer Writers' Colony and as finalist judge for the Langum Prize. He is the founding director of the Low-Residency MFA in Fiction and Nonfiction, and Professor of English Emeritus, at Southern New Hampshire University.

"The author's candor is both admirable and unsettling." —***Mercury Book Reviews***

"Begiebing seems intuitively right about the commonality of experience, the connection developed worlds apart by rough-shod children heading into the woods on a dangerous mission of freedom. Will this shared experience be there in quite the same form for another generation? Does it matter, after all? We have Begiebing's engaging memoir, if not to answer these questions, then at least to document their astonishing yet ordinary source." –"Into the Woods: Berkshire Boyhood" by Michael Shuman, *The Mailer Review* (Vol. 8, No. 1, Fall 2014, 411-17. The Norman Mailer Society)

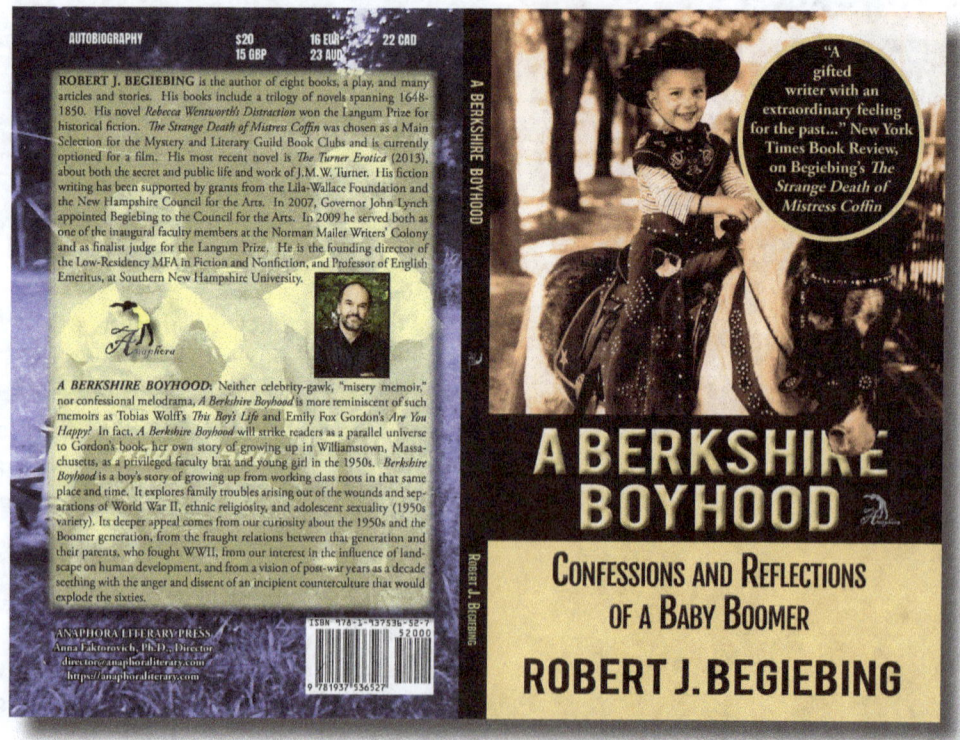

Memoirs of a Main Street Boy: Growing Up in America's Ancient City (230pp, 6X9", $35: Hardcover: ISBN-13: 978-1-68114-271-5; $20: Softcover: ISBN-13: 978-1-68114-272-2; $2.99: EBook: ISBN-13: 978-1-68114-273-9; LCCN: 2016941194; Memoir; Release: September 1, 2016): tells the tale of growing up at a tempestuous time in U.S. history—from the Great Depression, through World War II and the Cold War—in a town where America's colonial history was even more tempestuous, amid homes and institutions that still exist. The story takes you through the author's interplay with these historic places and events that helped shape U.S. history, as well as shaping his life and those of his generation.

Combines the story of Annapolis Maryland's unique place in American history with its typical small town life, made atypical by its Chesapeake Bay location and its unique institutions, such as the U.S. Naval Academy—wonderful playgrounds for a child of the mid-20th century. This is not an autobiography. It is a memoir of growing up in one of the country's most disruptive yet most dynamic eras—from the end of the Great Depression, through World War II to the Cold War.

"Book blends personal memories with small-town Annapolis' unique place in American history." –De Castillo, *Annapolis Patch*, September 16, 2016

RALPH W. CROSBY was a Washington Correspondent and magazine writer during the Eisenhower-Kennedy-Johnson era; culminating his journalistic career in 1972 as an editor with the Kiplinger organization. Currently, he is chairman of Crosby Marketing Communications, an award-winning advertising and public relations firm he founded in 1973. The firm, with 50-plus employees, has offices in Annapolis and Washington, D.C. Memoirs of a Main Street Boy is his third published book.

Still Rising from Ashes (Softcover: $20, 156pp, 6X9": ISBN: 978-1-68114-409-2; Hardcover: $35: ISBN-13: 978-1-68114-410-8; EBook: $2.99: ISBN-13: 978-1-68114-411-5; 2017918227; Edited by: Emily Mullaney; Biography & Autobiography—Personal Memoirs; Release: March 1, 2018): Charlene grew up poverty-stricken in the Bronx, New York. As a child, she bore witness to the streets decimating her family. Her mother's relationships with men turned abusive as her crack cocaine addiction grew. Her brothers traded their innocence for lives of crime, and church dances with child hood friends and neighborhood sweet hearts became nightclub shootings with gang bangers and bad boys. Anger burned in Charlene so blindingly, it led her to the same dark streets that sparked her rage in the first place. There would be much more pain before she'd find her way again, but the fire of faith burns brighter than that of anger. Soon, the poverty from whence Charlene came would be but ashes. Then, the real work would begin.

CHARLENE SWINTON-MATTOX is an author, TV personality, and model. After leaving New York, Charlene attended Central Connecticut State University where she majored in communications. She has since earned an MBA in Marketing, as well as a MA in Social Media Relations. Currently, Swinton-Mattox serves as a board member for the Spanish Speaking Center of New Britain. She resides in Connecticut with her husband of 26 years and their two children, along with two children for whom she serves as a foster parent.

"Recent Books of Interest to African American Scholars" — *Journal of Blacks in Higher Education*, March 14, 2018: includes a listing for Charlene Swinton-Mattox's *Still Rising*.

TEXTBOOKS

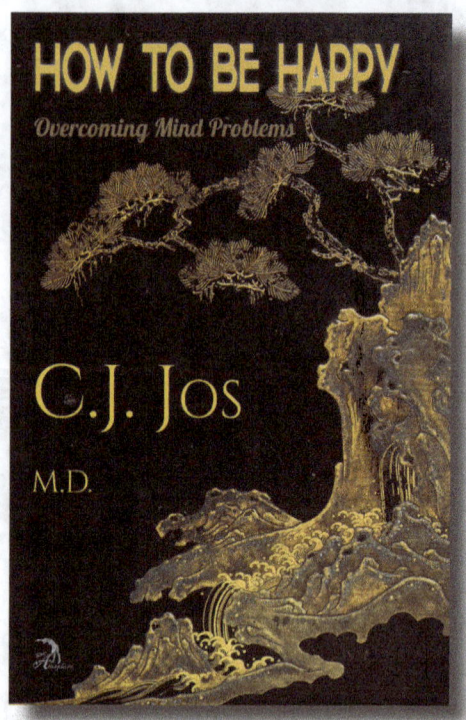

How to Be Happy: Overcoming Mind Problems: ($20, 224pp, 6X9": Softcover: ISBN: 978-1-68114-430-6; $35: Hardcover: ISBN: 978-1-68114-431-3; $2.99: EBook: ISBN: 978-1-68114-432-0; LCCN: 2018905513; Self-Help—Mood Disorders—Depression; Release: August 20, 2018): Everyone will readily agree that overcoming a mental illness is absolutely essential to be happy in life. This book takes it a step further, emphasizing that even *Mind Problems*, the more common psychological predicaments, though well below the clinical bar, can affect a person's thinking, behavior and wellbeing in profoundly negative ways and bring down the structure of harmony and health. The book is intended to educate the public on the importance of overcoming these problems by employing self-help strategies, psychotherapy, and, if needed, taking medications. For those concerned with overvaluing life's mundane problems, thus trivializing the real medical disorders, there are plenty of thought-provoking evidence throughout the book, to calm their nerves.

C.J. Jos, M.D.: is board-certified physician trained in Medicine, Neurology and Psychiatry, and currently a Professor at St Louis University, St Louis and a Medical Director at COMTREA, a large non-profit organization treating the ill children and adults. Dr. Jos is ideally suited to write this book, since during his long professional career, he has witnessed the limitations of Diagnostic Manuals and the intrinsic power of *Mind Problems* to erupt and disrupt human lives.

The History of British and American Author-Publishers ($20, 368pp, 6X9": Softcover: ISBN: 978-1-68114-373-6; $35: Hardcover: ISBN-13: 978-1-68114-374-3; $2.99: EBook: ISBN-13: 978-1-68114-375-0; LCCN: 2017950922; Edited by: Mallory Cormack; Includes bibliography and index; 11 illustrations; Biography & Autobiography—Editors, Journalists, Publishers; Release: January 5, 2018): This book describes the road some of the world's top authors took to self-publication. Charles Dickens self-published *A Tale of Two Cities* in his periodical, *All the Year Round*. Sir Walter Scott published most of his fiction and poetry with Constantine and Ballantyne, publishers in which he was heavily invested. Virginia and Leonard Woolf's Hogarth Press published nearly all of Virginia's writings; these works are still used by feminists and birthed the stream of consciousness movement (a style that was too unique for "mainstream" publishers). Herman Melville paid Harper $29,571 for 350 copies of Clarel. Mark Twain spent $1.3 million (in today's money) to print Old Times on the Mississippi with J. R. Osgood.

"If you are looking for a primer on the historical greats, advice on a thousand new non-fiction 'must read' topics to research on Wikipedia, or critical and solid advice on how to succeed via a non-conglomerate publishing avenue (by avoiding historic mistakes), you should look into snagging a copy of this. It is a bit depressing to identify with great authors by reading deep details of their pain and failures, but there is a degree of pity that once reached is actually quite inspiring." —***Toast Toasted***, Jason Brown

Research Writing About Cultural Artifacts: (Softcover: $15, 106pp, 6X9": ISBN: 978-1-68114-436-8; Hardcover: $30: ISBN: 978-1-68114-437-5; Ebook: $2.99: ISBN: 978-1-68114-438-2; LCCN: 2018906914; Edited by: Margaret Blatz; Release: October 22, 2018): Research writing courses in colleges across the world have a tendency to be dull, and similar to each other. They typically review the elements of the research paper and ask students to draft formulaic papers that fit the set guidelines. There have been plenty of textbooks written for these classes that repeat nearly identical information. This market is definitely over-saturated. One alternative is a Research Writing class that focuses on audio-visual entertainment (such as film or music) and other cultural artifacts, as well as diversity-related topics. This class offers more engaging topics for research than the repeating political or social topics that fit the formula of a traditional college research writing class. Students are likely to be more interested in researching films they watch for fun than dusty topics they are not personally invested in. More colleges are likely to start teaching these types of classes especially with help from textbooks like this one that suits this curriculum. American students are reading less, and watching media more, a class that accepts this shift can embrace the students' preferences, stimulating their imagination and desire to learn. This textbook combines the rigor of a Research Writing class with the imaginative and culturally significant realm of Cultural Studies. Concepts that are typically discussed in Research Writing textbooks, like close reading, thesis statement, and clichés, are covered in full. Complex rhetorical concepts are explained simply and fully. Additionally, the elements of a proper argument are not only digested for students, but are also assisted with discussions of political, economic, social and other types of cultural concepts such as communism or feminism. Teachers who are looking for ideas to inspire their plans, will find assignments across the book to utilize.

This book is deliberately short and meant to be a cheap paperback, so that it can be utilized as a quick reference guide and idea book for cultural studies related topics (if not as the primary textbook for a course that entirely combines Research Writing with Cultural Studies).

Introduction to Literature (Softcover: $20, 300pp, 6X9", ISBN: 978-1-68114-442-9; Hardcover: $35: ISBN: 978-1-68114-443-6; Ebook: $2.99: ISBN: 978-1-68114-444-3; LCCN: 2018906964; Edited by: Rebecca Baird; Language Arts & Disciplines—Reading Skills; Release: October 22, 2018): Within lies a shakeup of the traditional introductory literature course textbook formula, with a unique perspective on literature. You will find some theories that have not even been published in scholarly journals before, like the examination of the merchants' language that Swift uses to disguise his meaning. Each of the sections on fiction, drama and poetry provides the most essential commentary, definitions and concepts. The readings include three short stories from Edgar Allan Poe, novel segments from Don Quixote, and Gulliver's Travels, various poems, and a classic Greek play, Lysistrata. The uniting elements in these pieces are satire, sarcasm, and other forms of humor. This dense political, social and cultural content should inspire students with questions and a desire to write about it.

ANNA FAKTOROVICH is the Founder, Director, Designer and Editor-in-Chief of the Anaphora Literary Press. Faktorovich has also published two poetry collection, *Improvisational Arguments* (Fomite Press, 2011) and *Battle for Athens* (Anaphora, 2012), as well as scholarly books with McFarland: *Rebellion as Genre* (February, 2013) and *Formulas of Popular Fiction* (August 2014). Faktorovich worked as a full-time college professor for over four years. She has a Ph.D. in English Literature.

Essays in Innovative Risk Management Methods: Based on Deterministic, Stochastic and Quantum Approaches ($15, 64pp, 6X9"; ISBN: 978-1-68114-451-1; $30: ISBN: 978-1-68114-452-8; $2.99: ISBN: 978-1-68114-453-5; LCCN: 2018907298; Edited by: Julie Wong Shi; October 1, 2018): This analysis works towards overcoming the current business valuation logic as prevalently set by banks and other credit entities or, more generally, within risk capital markets. Current banking practice applies rigorous deterministic valuations that are based entirely on indices and ratios. Present accounting models are also poor representations of the correct money-credit-production-income mechanisms. This research proposes reforms for methods of business evaluation and determining the relative solidity or probability of insolvency. Each of the themes treated has its own identity, however they are integrated in relation to problems related to bank risk management and relevant creditworthiness assessments.

MARCO DESOGUS has a PhD in Economics, and specializes in microcredit, public administrations and cooperative companies. He works as a credit financial advisor while conducting independent economic studies. His publications include *Introduzione all'economia umanistica* (Ibiskos Editrice Risolo, 2015), and *Microfinanza e microcredito: definizioni ed analisi di sviluppo in ambiente teorico quantico della produzione. Scenari italiani e prospettive possibili* (ilmiolibro: L'Espresso-Feltrinelli, 2014). Desogus also works with local and international journals as an author and referee.

ELISA CASU holds a BSc in Economics. She is an expert in banking, accounting systems and mathematical modeling for business, finance and credit. Casu works as a business consultant, dealing especially in planning and control, business analysis and due diligence. She frequently speaks at conferences and seminars in these fields.

The Encyclopedic Philosophy of Michel Serres: Writing The Modern World and Anticipating the Future: ($20, 280pp, 6X9", ISBN-13: 978-1-68114-234-0, August 2016): This monograph represents the first comprehensive study dedicated to the interdisciplinary French philosopher Michel Serres. As the title of this project unequivocally suggests, Serres's prolific body of work paints a rending portrait of what it means for a sentient being to live in the modern world. This book reflects Serres's profound conviction that "philosopher c'est anticiper"/ 'to philosophize (about something) is to anticipate' ("Philosophie Magazine"). According to Serres, a philosopher is someone who possesses an extremely broad base of knowledge coupled with the uncanny ability to envision what might transpire based upon his or her astute observations concerning phenomena that are already starting to unfold in a given society. From 1968 to the present, Serres has been generating forceful, "prophetic" visions in his works that mingle philosophy, religion, theology, contemporary science, and literature.

KEITH MOSER is Associate Professor of French at Mississippi State University. He is the author of four other books including *A Practical Guide to French Harki Literature, J.M.G. Le Clézio: A Concerned Citizen of the Global Village, J.M.G. Le Clézio dans la forêt des paradoxes* (co-editor with Bruno Thibault), and *'Privileged Moments' in the Novels and Short Stories of J.M.G. Le Clézio: His Contemporary Development of a Traditional French Literary Device.* Moser has also contributed approximately forty essays to peer-reviewed publications such as *The French Review.*

"A thorough and relevant examination… anyone that has an interest in Serres will find the book stimulating and enjoying." —Eileen M. Angelini, Canisius College, United States, *South Atlantic Review*

NOVELS

The Visit (Softcover: $20, 182pp, 6X9⬛: 978-1-68114-353-8; Hardcover: $35: 978-1-68114-354-5; EBook: $2.99: 978-1-68114-355-2; LCCN: 2017944015; Historical Fiction; Release Date: November 7, 2017): The frantic preparations for the visit of John Fitzgerald Kennedy to his hometown in Ireland are largely seen through the eyes of Martin Moroney and Eileen Blayney who are beginning to fall in love.

The Mayor of the town, New Ross, has to use all of his considerable skills to keep a sense of order and decorum. He knows that the eyes of the world will be on them. An aggressive CIA advance party causes much grief and forces the Town Council to change its plans for 'security' reasons.

The events are keenly observed by Martin and Eileen who "come of age" against the background of the visit. In a sense, the town itself begins to come of age.

The world's press begins to arrive. Four days before the visit a man checks into the local hotel and registers under the name of L.H. Oswald.

Despite many difficulties, the visit is an outstanding success. Like the return of Ulysses, it is the stuff of myth.

Five months later, JFK is assassinated in Dallas. The town goes into mourning and Martin and Eileen are forced to confront newly-awakened demons.

Michael G. Casey: educated in Cambridge University where he earned a Ph.D. He worked mainly in the Irish public sector. He has published a novel, Come Home, Robbie, a book of non-fiction, Ireland's Malaise, and an award-winning chapbook of short fiction, Treadmill. Several of his individual short stories and poems have won awards, international and domestic.

Massage World: The Novel (Softcover: $20, 266p, 6X9": ISBN: 978-1-68114-469-6; Hardcover: $35: ISBN: 978-1-68114-470-2; EBook: $2.99: ISBN: 978-1-68114-471-9; LCCN: 2018954819; Fiction—Thrillers—Crime; Edited by: Danielle Willett; Release: November 8, 2018): The body is in pain. So around the world the massage industry is booming, from ubiquitous airport massage bars and upscale spas to risqué outcall and down-market parlors. Enter into these pages massage therapist Ingrid Swanson's mission to open a grandiose health spa, Massage World, against the wishes of a wild parlor lord. The all-too cunning antagonist Jack Cobb dispatches a corrupt undercover vice detective to solicit unlawful massages transcribed in delirious police reports. Cobb goes on to manipulate zany media coverage, which incites a rollicking raid of the premises and neighborhood organizations to picket and protest so he can take over Massage World. Until the cavalry comes in the form of a lesbian biker gang… The war of the sexes writ large.

Eric Madeen's writings have appeared in such diverse publications as Time, Asia Week, The East, Daily Yomiuri, Tokyo Journal, Kyoto Journal, Mississippi Review, Japanophile and All Nippon Airways' WINGSPAN, to which he contributed several feature stories. His first novel, Tanga, was inspired by a two-year stint in the Peace Corps in Gabon, Africa and garnered nominations for AWP and L.A. Arts Council awards. He is currently associate professor of modern American literature at Tokyo City University and adjunct professor at Keio University. His website is at ericmadeen.com.

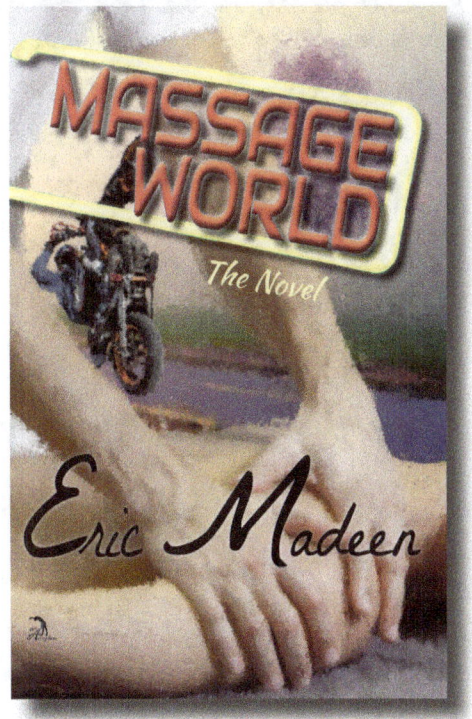

Bluebird (Softcover: $20: ISBN: 978-1-68114-445-0; Hardcover: $35: ISBN: 978-1-68114-446-7; Ebook: $2.99: ISBN: 978-1-68114-447-4; LCCN: 2018907159; Fiction—Literary; Edited by Kristen Cole; Release: October 1, 2018): is the story of a man turning to stone. Following his young son's death, Henry Dunstan yearns to become insentient and impervious to sorrow. He turns to boulders, marble, and flint to gain wisdom, guided by a decades-old vision he experienced while visiting with a carnival psychic in St. Louis.

MICHAEL SMITH is a writer and Francophile residing in Salt Lake City, Utah. His short works of fiction and creative non-fiction have appeared in *The Hopper, The Los Angeles Review of Los Angeles, The Baltimore Review, The Delmarva Review, Bacopa Literary Review, Drunk Monkeys, Blue Lake Review,* and other literary journals. Michael is a recent Pushcart Prize nominee.

Charlton's Ground (Softcover: $20, 232pp, 6X9": ISBN: 978-1-68114-460-3; Hardcover: $35: ISBN: 978-1-68114-461-0; EBook: $2.99: ISBN: 978-1-68114-462-7; LCCN: 2018907740; Release: January 15, 2019; Edited by Destany Atkinson; Fiction—Historical—General): Charlton is born into slavery on a South Carolina plantation in 1837. Belle, the master's daughter, intervenes to save the tiny baby's life when her father contemplates killing off the runt. Belle's relationship with Charlton progresses from nurturer to teacher to friend to childhood love. She promises to marry him if she can use the words of the Declaration of Independence to convince their master that Charlton has rights. These events sets him on an irrevocable course to understanding the vicious and unjust world of the American South, where innocent childhood dreams lead to unthinkable cruelty.

DAN CASSENTI is the author of The Mental Representation of Goals (VDM-Verlag), a non-fiction research study. He earned his Ph.D. in cognitive psychology from Penn State and uses the insights from his education to give his characters mental depth and richness. He lives in Maryland, the home state of his two greatest heroes, Frederick Douglass and Harriet Tubman, who risked their lives to defend the rights of others.

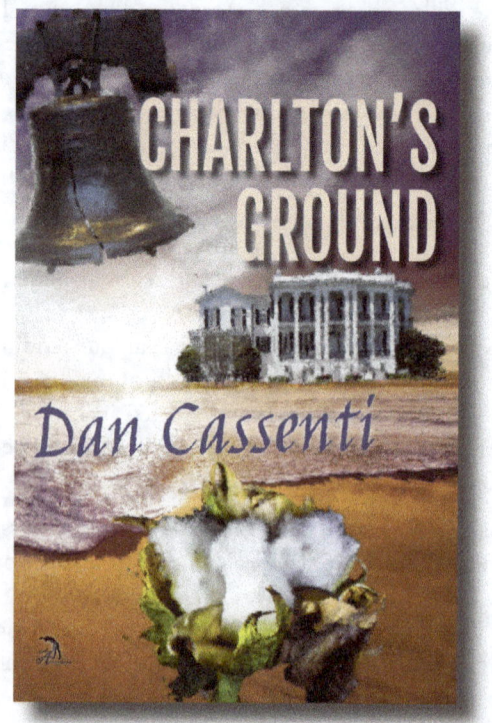

Bedfellows ($15, 116pp, 6X9□: Softcover: ISBN: 978-1-68114-376-7; $30: Hardcover: ISBN-13: 978-1-68114-377-4; $2.99: EBook: ISBN: 978-1-68114-378-1; LCCN: 2017954087; Romance—Action & Adventure; Release: January 1, 2018): What does a South Florida philosophy professor turned car salesman do when he can't fall out of love with a passionate, smart, witty, sexy redneck gal who just can't stay faithful? What do you do when the yearning melancholy animal overtakes the man of reason? Jackson and Annette get to the heart of the matter when she has to travel up to the Alabama panhandle to pay a last visit to her beloved, dying, wickedly rambunctious grandmother Estelle. Seeing Annette attached to a likely man, her kin go in cahoots to see if they can engineer a wedding between tempestuous Annette and her laid-back but anxious suitor. Along the way there is a funeral to be held, fishing and hunting to be done, liquor to be drunk and canasta to be played. Jackson is a stranger in a strange but friendly land. Can the family tame Annette's wild and stubborn ways enough to make her see that Jackson might be the man of her dreams?

JOHNNY **P**AYNE'S books include the poetry collections *Heaven of Ashes* and *Vassal* and the novels *Kentuckiana, Second Chance,* and *La Muerte de Papi.* He directs the MFA Program in Creative Writing at Mount Saint Mary's University in Los Angeles. He and his collaborator Kimo Oades, who together created the VR game *Odyssey,* are currently at work on a novel set in Imperial China, *The Eunuch's Song,* which will partly take place in virtual reality.

"This is a delicious odyssey through a land of friendship, kinfolk, and an unquenchable desire for a woman Jackson just can't get off his mind." —J. Bradley Minnick, Host Arts & Letters Radio, *NPR*

The Art of the Law: A Novel (Softcover: $20, 276pp, 6X9": ISBN: 978-1-68114-448-1; Hardcover with flaps: $35: ISBN: 978-1-68114-449-8; EBook: $2.99: ISBN: 978-1-68114-450-4; LCCN: 2018907299; Release: October 15, 2018; Fiction—Thrillers—Legal): Nevin Montgomery, a young lawyer with a prestigious Boston law firm, is dispatched to the Cape Cod compound of Andrew Windsor, the most acclaimed artist in America, to update Windsor's will. Nevin arrives to the news that a woman who had secretly modeled for Windsor for decades has been found dead. Nevin, who is battling a hidden drug addiction, is asked to remain at the Windsor compound to complete his assignment because the health of his law firm's most famous client is deteriorating rapidly. Nevin is introduced to the secretive art world, and he becomes smitten along the way with Catina Cruz, a beautiful young Portuguese-American woman he meets at the compound. Nevin eventually learns that Catina models for James Windsor, Andrew Windsor's son. James is a painter in his own right, albeit not nearly of the stature of his father. When Andrew Windsor finally dies, a will contest ensues. At Andrew's request, Nevin had cut Andrew's wife and son out of the will and they challenge the will in court. Nevin is instructed by his law firm to defend the will, but he has some further investigating to do before he can: investigating that reveals more than he ever wanted to know about the woman he has come to love… and about himself.

SCOTT **D**OUGLAS **G**ERBER is a law professor at Ohio Northern University and an associated scholar at Brown University's Political Theory Project. His eight previous books include, most recently, *Mr. Justice: A Novel.*

"A legal thriller that truly is… a thriller, a will contest that proves to be an extraordinary contest of… wills, flawed ones at that." —Ronald S. Barak, author of *The Puppet Master* and *The Amendment Killer,* Brooks/Lotello thrillers

Mendelssohn & Co.: A Fictive Memoir ($20, 150pp, 6X9": Softcover: ISBN: 978-1-68114-427-6; $35: Hardcover: ISBN: 978-1-68114-428-3; $2.99: EBook: ISBN: 978-1-68114-429-0; LCCN: 2018905378; Fiction—Historical—General; Release: August 15, 2018): The early nineteenth-century German composers and pianists Felix Mendelssohn and his sister Fanny Hensel are familiar to many people, but few are aware of their younger siblings, Rebecka and Paul. *Mendelssohn & Co.* is an imagined portrait of this gifted Berlin family, whose lives were shaped by crucial developments in German culture and politics. It is told in the first person, through the eyes and memories of the youngest child, Paul, a gifted amateur cellist and a Berlin banker in the family firm of Mendelssohn & Co. Though Paul's youth is overshadowed by the early fame of the musical prodigies, he outlives his three siblings and becomes a quiet mainstay of his extended family. After the premature deaths of Fanny and Felix in 1847, Paul struggles to protect their legacies and to guide their orphaned sons. His story is closely based on the historical record, but the scenes and dialogues Paul reconstructs are fictional, as are many of his private thoughts and meditations.

During her career as an English professor, ROSEMARIE BODENHEIMER specialized in Victorian and Modern novels and autobiographies. Fascinated by the links between a writer's letters and fiction, she developed a form of textual biographical criticism in books about George Eliot and Charles Dickens. At retirement, she explored an unusual archive of family letters and journals that led to a book about her parents and grandparents, who fled Hitler's Germany in the early 1930s to build new lives in the United States. Mendelssohn & Co. continues her practice of weaving stories from letters, biography and history, and extends her focus on German Jewish lives back into the 19th century. Attempting to bring the Mendelssohn family dynamics to life, she took a new turn into biographical fiction, and drew on her experience as an amateur cellist and chamber musician.

The Second of Seven: A Novel (Softcover: $20: ISBN: 978-1-68114-421-4; Hardcover: $35: ISBN-13: 978-1-68114-422-1; EBook: $2.99: ISBN-13: 978-1-68114-423-8; LCCN: 2018904275; Apocalyptic & Post-Apocalyptic; Edited by Alicia Jacques and Joseph Foster; Release: July 26, 2018): Military contractor, Abram Jacobson, is tasked with returning to the third dimension to prevent the Red Mage from crossing sides and obliterating all life in the seven dimensions. Unlike his first visit to the Third, Abram is assigned a small team to assist him. They cross over but barely a day goes by before his first teammate dies. Disaster follows Abram and his team at every turn, and certain doom looms on the horizon when they are told the Red Mage has already crossed to their home. Abram is granted precious little time to bathe in the magical arts of the Third in an attempt to save all life in the aggregate dimensions. Despite his newfound abilities, he soon realizes that the Red Mage's forces are too powerful to defeat using righteous tactics alone. With everything he values in jeopardy, Abram's darker side surfaces, demonstrating that he is capable of far viler things than he had ever imagined.

JEREMIE GUY graduated from Towson University with an English degree and a creative writing minor. He has written and edited freelance for a number of organizations, and he sometimes dabbles as a ghostwriter for fiction and nonfiction. He has won first place in a handful of writing contests, and his creative works have appeared in a variety publications, including an appearance in Earthbound Fiction's short story anthology *Dark Stars*. He is a member of Lambda Iota Tau, international literary honors society.

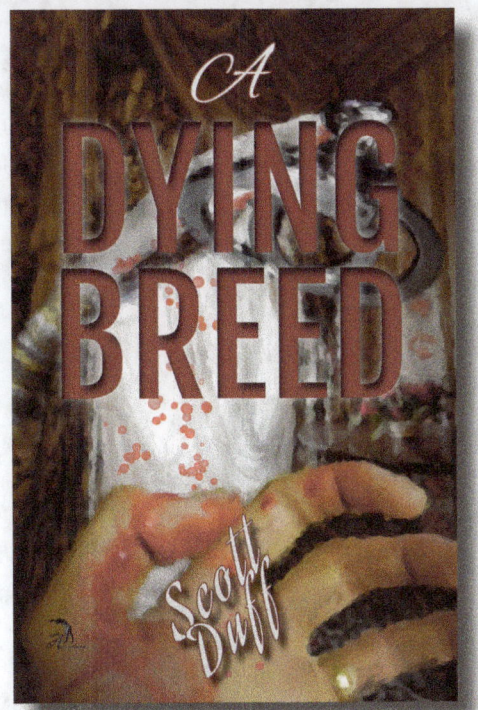

A Dying Breed ($20, 130pp, 6X9": Softcover: 978-1-68114-406-1; $35: Cloth Hardcover: 978-1-68114-407-8; $2.99: EBook: 978-1-68114-407-8; LCCN: 2017917815; Edited by Codi Reynolds; Release: February 25, 2018): Michael is an attractive, athletic, widower police officer with two wonderful small children. Michael serendipitously crosses paths with a new type of serial killer who is good looking, highly intelligent, highly trained when it comes to fighting, and deeply believes that everything he does is for a greater good. Michael unexpectedly finds love with a beautiful young woman named Bailey who somehow gets intertwined in his dealings when it comes to this charismatic murderer. Michael must find a way to defeat both his own personal demons and those belonging to this unique form of evil as he is forced to watch Bailey succumb to horrific acts of mutilation. Michael and Bailey both share extremely passionate and intimate moments in the most beautiful and dazzling of backdrops, but this only makes it more difficult for Michael to keep his emotions in check as he attempts to help Bailey overcome the atrocities inflicted by this most iniquitous of criminals.

"'Great Book really enjoyed it. Great talent. Eagerly awaiting your next release.'" —Mary Hall Cochran, "Capitol Police Officer Pens Crime Novel" by Rusty Marks, January 28, 2018, *West Virginia News*

SCOTT DUFF was raised alone by a single mother and is a graduate of the West Virginia State Police Academy. He has been a police officer for twenty years and has even performed as an undercover officer within a drug task force. Scott is married to a gorgeous wife and has two grown children. This is Scott's first book, with several more in the works.

Book Trailer: https://youtu.be/kNeGsJ4UYTs

Lucky Dick: A Novel-in-Stories (Softcover: $20, 126pp, 6X9": ISBN: 978-1-68114-400-9; Hardcover: $35: ISBN-13: 978-1-68114-401-6; EBook: $2.99: ISBN-13: 978-1-68114-402-3; LCCN: 2017915857; Fiction—Action & Adventure; Edited by: Shauneice Robinson; Release: January 20, 2018): When young biker "Lucky Dick" Richards first agreed to help steal $4,000 in OxyContin he thought it would be a quick way to score some pills and cash. But once he is abandoned by his best friend and on the run with nothing separating him from homelessness but his motorcycle, he discovers it was anything but quick. With nowhere left to go but forward, Lucky strikes west leaving his friends, family, and enemies to deal with the wreckage left behind. Told from multiple perspectives, this novel-in-stories is a gritty and poetic look at the American landscape and one man's discovery of what an outlaw's freedom actually entails.

ROD DIXON'S short-stories have appeared in several journals such as CC&D, Revolution John, and Red Rock Review. He is the former non-fiction editor of the now defunct Ontologica: A Journal of Art and Thought. He researches and develops manufacturing procedures for a non-profit serving the blind and visually impaired. He lives in Kentucky with his two children.

Guantanamo Redux ($15: Softcover ISBN-13: 978-1-68114-299-9; $30: Hardcover ISBN-13: 978-1-68114-300-2; $2.99: EBook ISBN-13: 978-1-68114-301-9; LCCN: 2016919184; Release: April 15, 2017): uses the techniques of speculative fiction and science fiction to create a dystopian vision of the near future in America. Here, most any kind of dissent is criminalized and individuals are routinely charged with terrorism offences. The L. A. Mercy Killer is incarcerated in the Bay of Frisco, a center for domestic terrorists, after the *third terror* has destroyed much of Los Angeles. Special Agent Orwell and Judge Dan believe the girl whose face you can't see was deeply involved in not only the Mercy Killer's crime, but, also, the massive terror attack on Los Angeles. In Part II of the novella, a flashback, we retrace the steps of the girl whose face you can't see prior to the *third terror*. Who is she and what does she represent? Did she know the L.A. Mercy Killer?

DEAN GESSIE enjoyed a long career as Head of the English Department at Pickering College in Newmarket, Ontario. While there, he was also Director of the award-winning Joshua Weinzweig Creative Writing Program. As a teenager, Gessie's play won best entry for Northern Ontario in the Canadian Broadcasting Corporation's playwriting contest. Gessie also won Honorable Mention in the 2008 Press 53 Novella Competition. Most recently, one of Gessie's short stories was selected to the list of Highly Commended Stories in the international Manchester Fiction Prize, England's biggest literary award for unpublished creative writing. Gessie has also written and served extensively as a social justice activist.

"Gessie evokes a nightmare scenario of an Orwellian government under which justice, freedom, and equality are antiquated notions, and you can hear 'amendments of the Constitution snapping like tracheal bones…' The message is timely and pertinent." —*Publishers Weekly*, April 2017

TrumpeterVille (Softcover: $15, 46pp, 6X9⊠: ISBN: 978-1-68114-379-8; Hardcover: $30: ISBN-13: 978-1-68114-380-4; EBook: $2.99: ISBN-13: 978-1-68114-381-1; LCCN: 2017954155; Satirical Novella; Release: December 15, 2017): is animal allegory in the tradition of *Animal Farm* by George Orwell. The story reflects American political culture before and during the presidency of Donald Trump. The new leader of the lake nation of Swanville, simply called the Trumpeter, promises an ambitious agenda. He will dismantle the Swan Care Act of his predecessor, President Lulu. He will drain the Swamp where the left wing oligarchy eat the very best protein and vegetation. He will increase shoreline habitat by bringing down the beaver wall on the North River. And he will ban migratory birds from Swanville because they are looters and moochers and not part of the Great Swan's plan. Eventually, the new president becomes cob-in-chief of a nation at war with its neighbors and itself. *TrumpeterVille* is political satire that wags a cautionary tale.

A Brief History of Summer Employment (\$15: Softcover ISBN-13: 978-1-68114-338-5; \$30: Hardcover ISBN: 978-1-68114-339-2; \$2.99: EBook ISBN-13: 978-1-68114-340-8; LCCN: 2017940877; Fiction—Literary; Release: November 1, 2017): is a fictional memoir that unpacks blood sport in the marketplace. The narrator finances many years of post-secondary education by taking summer jobs of dizzying variety. As he documents his experiences, he becomes *porte-parole* for a generation in the grips of precarious work. More broadly, however, he illuminates personalities of intriguing emotional and psychological complexity in circumstances that are obviously or discreetly desperate. These are dispatches from the front lines, stories that present an ironic and critical portrait of economic activity and human imperfections. Adversity and anguish burn in the atmosphere as do humor and heroism. The workplace is a dangerous environment to earn a living.

Fabrications: (\$15, Print ISBN: 978-1-68114-085-8, EBook ISBN: 978-1-681140-86-5, LCCN: 2015904378, 64pp, 6X9", April 2015): is a spritely love story that in its odd way recapitulates Henry James's *The Wings of the Dove*. A young man and a young woman are in love but don't have the financial resources they know they will need not just to be comfortable but to avoid the resentment either one would feel about having made a great sacrifice for their lives together. In James's story, Merton Densher married a wealthy young woman at death's door so he can inherit the money he needs in order to marry Kate Croy. Here, it is Nadine, the starlet, who marries the elderly producer with heart troubles, so that she and Abner, the writer, can look forward to a life of comfort and ease. Slavitt notices what James didn't, or couldn't in 1902—that the situation is inherently comic. And he has written a novel that is sprightlier than its model but, because of its humor, closer to the texture of life.

DAVID R. SLAVITT: educated at Andover, Yale, and Columbia, is the author of more than 115 books—novels, poetry, reportage, and translations. He was the movie reviewer for *Newsweek* in the sixties and was co-editor of the *Johns Hopkins Complete Roman Drama* as well as the *Penn Complete Greek Drama*. Among his recent publications: T*he Sonnets and Short Poems of Francesco Petrarch* (2012, Harvard University Press), *Civil Wars* (2013, Louisiana State University Press), and *The Four Other Plays of Sophocles* (2013 Johns Hopkins University Press).

Fireworks: ($20, ISBN: 978-1-937536-92-3, $35: Hardcover ISBN: 978-1-68114-121-3, 6X9", 180pp, February 2015): two women are thrown into the Hezbollah Israel war of 2006. Angie is thirty, a nurse from Kansas, in Beirut for the summer to get away from a broken heart. Zahra is a sixteen year old Shiite, on summer break and in love for the first time. Through terror, loss, grief, self-forgiveness and the workings of a local doctor, the two women move from despair to grace and to the long-awaited shore.

Sarah Houssayni was born in Beirut, Lebanon, she moved to upstate NY at the age of 25 to complete her training in Pediatrics. She lives in Wichita, Kansas where she raises two boys and is a clinical assistant professor at Kansas University. She has published *Narratives in Family Medicine, Survive and Thrive, The Examined Life* and *Pulse Voices*. She is a Writer's Digest Award Winner for Personal Essay, this is her first book.

"*Fireworks* illuminates the complexity of religious codes and cultural boundaries. From Kansas City to Beirut, Houssayni's characters navigate family tension, political unrest, and unexamined grief. This is a writer full of curiosity and courage." –Christine Hemp, award winning poet and NPR host, www.christinehemp.com

"This story could not be more timely. The breadth of Houssayni's empathetic imagination in *Fireworks* is impressive; the writing is sensitive to difference in the best sense." —Charles Holdefer, *The Contractor*

"Sarah Houssayni's *Fireworks* delivers a vivid and rewarding tale. From Kansas City to New York City, to Beirut, Houssayni's debut encompasses and transcends the known world through characters that are fully fleshed and deftly wrought." —Juliet Patterson, *The Truant Lover* and *Dirge*

Forever Gentleman: ($40, cloth hardcover, 472pp, 6X9"; ISBN: 978-1-68114-229-6; Edited by Sofia Nehlawi; July 2016): Written in a nineteenth-century style, a sweeping saga of suspense, romance, mystery, and music. Travel back in time and experience Victorian London at its best and worst—a city of beauty and brilliance, and a city steeped in filth and despair. Meet Nathan Sinclair, a struggling young architect and gifted pianist who lives in two vastly different worlds, mingling in high society while dwelling in suffocating debt and poverty. While performing at a gathering of London's elite, Nathan meets Jocelyn Charlesworth, a breathtakingly beautiful but temperamental celebrity heiress. He is smitten, though she publicly humiliates him; their paths will intersect again in a most shocking manner.

Meanwhile, Nathan makes the acquaintance of Regina Lancaster, a woman of remarkable inner beauty, despite her pedestrian appearance. He must decide whether to follow his heart and pursue Regina, or flee England altogether to avoid imprisonment from a miserly creditor.

Roland Colton was awarded a bachelor's degree from the University of Utah and a juris doctorate from the University of San Diego School of Law. He has had a long career as a litigator and trial attorney. Trained in his youth as a classical pianist, he is a frequent performer at public and private gatherings. He also possesses a passion for architecture and the French language. Colton lives with his family in Southern California and France.

Shadows of an Empress ($20, 310pp, 6X9", Paperback: ISBN-13: 978-1-68114-263-0; $35: Hardcover ISBN 978-1-68114-282-1; $2.99: EBook ISBN 978-1-68114-283-8; LCCN: 2016905920; Release: June 22, 2016): When a recurring dream about a city she can't identify leaves Sylvia feeling unsettled and restless, she suddenly awakens one night to find the Empress Elisabeth of Austria, dressed in black, sitting in her living room. Suspecting their lives are somehow linked, but unable to find the answers in Sylvia's daily life, they embark on a whirlwind tour of places related to the empress's past, this time led by Sissi, Elisabeth's younger version. Along the way, the Archduchess Sophie arranges a courtship between Sylvia and Franz Joseph, a heart-broken Heinrich Heine laments the empress's tendency to credit him for her awful poetry, and Sigmund Freud offers commentary on their journey.

A creative writing professor at California University of Pennsylvania, **CAROLE WATERHOUSE** is the author of two previous novels, *The Tapestry Baby*, and *Without Wings*, as well as a short story collection, *The Paradise Ranch*. Her short stories have appeared in numerous literary magazines, including T*he Massachusetts Review, Crack the Spine, Crossconnect*, and *Turnrow*.

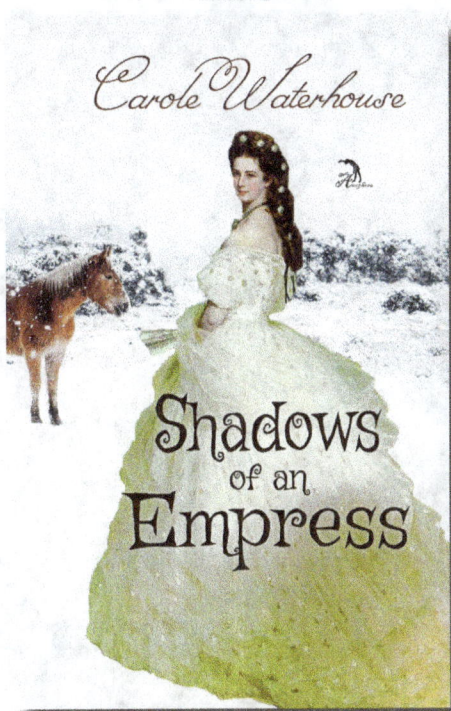

Myths & Ms. ($15, 102pp, 6X9": Softcover: ISBN: 978-1-68114-382-8; $30: Hardcover: ISBN: 978-1-68114-383-5; $2.99: EBook: ISBN: 978-1-68114-384-2; LCCN: 2017954173; Author Photo by Lora Brody; Edited by Shauneice Robinson; Mystical Play; Release: February 15, 2018): A ghost hovers watching and waiting to embody itself in the most auspicious womb. Its goal is to fulfill what it couldn't in its last lifetime called "soul work." *Myths & Ms.* is an intergenerational play about abortion and reincarnation, dramatizing the changing attitudes and conditions towards abortion in the 20th and 21st centuries. This idea of reincarnation highlights the strident voices from the pro-choice and pro-life camps.

ROSIE ROSENZWEIG, Resident Scholar in the Brandeis University Women's Studies Research Center, is also a Boston theatre reviewer. Her travel memoir, *A Jewish Mother in Shangri-la,* explores her son's introduction to his Buddhist teachers in America, France, India and Nepal. This exploration began her studies in Buddhist and Jewish meditation. Her published articles and poems have appeared in numerous anthologies and publications about these topics and the role of women in contemporary life.

"Rosie dives into complex cultural, moral, and spiritual topics with a loud, clear voice. Her characters are interesting and well-developed. This is an intergenerational story relevant to today's politics of gender and a women's right to choose." —Martha Joy Rose, Founder of the Museum of Motherhood

Dark Knowledge (Softcover: $20, 234pp, 6X9": 978-1-68114-367-5; Hardcover: $35: 978-1-68114-368-2; EBook: $2.99: 978-1-68114-369-9; LCCN: 2017911487; Historical Novel; Release: January 5, 2018): New York City, late 1860s. When young Chris Harmony learns that members of his family may have been involved in the illegal pre-Civil War slave trade, taking slaves from Africa to Cuba, he is appalled. Determined to learn the truth, he begins an investigation that takes him into a dingy waterfront saloon, musty old maritime records that yield startling secrets, and elegant brownstone parlors that may have been furnished by the trade. Since those once involved dread exposure, he meets denials and evasions, then threats, and a key witness is murdered. Chris has vivid fantasies of the suffering slaves on the ships and their savage revolts. How could seemingly respectable people be involved in so abhorrent a trade, and how did they avoid exposure? And what price must Chris pay to learn the painful truth and proclaim it?

CLIFFORD BROWDER is a writer living in New York. He has published a critical study of the Surrealist author André Breton, and biographies of the Wall Street financier Daniel Drew and the notorious abortionist Madame Restell. A collection of posts from his blog, *No Place for Normal: New York/ Stories from the Most Exciting City in the World* (Mill City Press, 2015), won first place in the Travel category of the 2015-2016 Reader Views Literary Awards; the Tenth Annual National Indie Excellence Award for Regional Non-Fiction; and Honorable Mention in the Culture category of the Eric Hoffer Book Awards for 2016.

"This was an excellent book. I really enjoyed reading about the history of the American illegal slave trade. Overall this novel is worth reading and I highly recommend it." —Nicole Williamson, April 11, 2018, *Midwest Book Review*

Make Dust Our Paper: A Novel ($20, 122pp, 6X9": Softcover: ISBN-13: 978-1-68114-335-4; $35: Hardcover: ISBN: 978-1-68114-336-1; $2.99: EBook: ISBN-13: 978-1-68114-337-8; LCCN: 2017905789; Fiction—Literary; Release: July 20, 2017): Carrigan approaches the millennium New Year craving climax and culmination. What he finds instead is constant anti-climax, and lack of definitional consequence for his failures and failings and genius. A conceptual heir to Fitzgerald's *This Side of Paradise*, this novel explores everything from Carrigan's past in the spelling bee as a contemptuous 12-year-old, to his father's death in Ireland years before, to the depth of mystery, violence, and secrecy that he returns to, both existentially, and literally, as he becomes 21, and then 22, without proper fanfare or notice.

JOSEPH M. REYNOLDS did his graduate work in Creative Fiction under the tutelage of acclaimed novelist and memoirist Da Chen. He teaches college in New England, and at Trinity College Dublin in Ireland during the summer term. As an undergraduate, he was a speechwriter and intern in the U.S. Senate office of the late Senator Edward M. Kennedy.

"An instant classic. A major new talent has arrived." —*Da Chen, New York Times best-selling author* and former recipient of *The Washington Post* best book award

"…The chapter written from Liam Keating's perspective is truly fantastic and worthy of its own book… In the space of one night, the fragility of John became clear. His façade had a spotlight shown on him, his character grows and you can see light in the cracks of his shell as the flesh beneath expands. A single night with his mother and a surprise interaction with his dead father is all it takes for his complexity to begin unraveling. ****" —*Toast Toasted*, Jason Brown, July 20, 2017

Vovochka: The True Confessions of Vladimir Putin's Best Friend and Confidant: ($20, 152pp, 6X9", Print ISBN: 978-1-68114-201-2, EBook ISBN: 978-1-68114-202-9, LCCN: 2015915059, October 2015): Welcome to Vladimir Putin's phantasmagoric world, where a heady mixture of Orthodoxy, socialism, imperialism, racism, homophobia, and Mother Russia worship defines and distorts reality. Vovochka is the story of "Vovochka" Putin and his intimate friend—a KGB agent with the same nickname. The two Vovochkas recruit informers in Berlin's gay bars, spy on East German dissidents, survive the trauma of the Soviet Union's collapse, fight American, Ukrainian, Jewish, and Estonian "fascists," and plot to restore Russia's power and glory. As their mindset assumes increasingly bizarre forms, Vovochka Putin experiences bouts of self-doubt that culminate in a weeklong cure in North Korea. A savage satire, Vovochka is also a terrifyingly plausible account of Vladimir Putin's evolution from a minor KGB agent in East Germany to the self-styled Savior and warmongering leader of a paranoid state.

ALEXANDER J. MOTYL'S artwork has been displayed in shows in New York, Philadelphia, and Toronto and is part of the permanent collection of the Ukrainian Museum in New York and the Ukrainian Cultural and Educational Centre in Winnipeg. He teaches at Rutgers University-Newark and is the author of six academic books, many articles.

"Buy the Book: Russia's Macho Leader Exposed: Motyl's story succeeds on two levels: it overlays actual events with a slightly skewed fictional story, and it exploits the bombast of Russian officialdom by pretending to take it seriously. The result is a parody in the great tradition of free expression." —*The American Spectator*

"Drips with veracity, with the truth of today's Russia. Nothing funny here. The tsar has returned from the grave. Only a miracle can prevent Russia and its people from sliding back to its deep-rooted ways." —Myron Kuropas, *The Ukrainian Weekly*

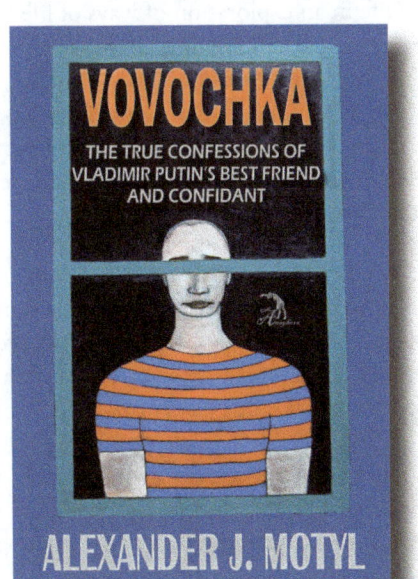

* 2016 *Foreword Indies Finalist: Humor* (Adult Fiction): "A satirical novel that illuminates injustices"

*Finalist in Gival Press' 2015 novel competition

Something Is Rotten in Fettig: ($20, 268pp, 6X9", Print ISBN: 978-1-68114-197-8, EBook ISBN: 978-1-68114-198-5; LCCN: 2015949531, February 2016): Told in a wry, understated voice, the novel satirizes the travails of Leopold Plotkin, a failing kosher butcher with a pathological aversion to conflict. After Plotkin commits an act that ignites a crisis in his Republic, he is propelled into conflicts with every branch of government. When he refuses the government's demands to undo what he did, he is indicted by a Secret Blind Jury, arrested by the National Constabulary, and consigned to the notorious Purgatory House of Detention, where he languishes next to a defrocked insane lawyer whose nocturnal machinations threaten to drive him crazy.

"…The uproarious novel is first and foremost a comedy, rife with absurdist humor…[e]nough jabs at law and criminal justice to make a point, all packaged in a courtroom drama that's pure entertainment." —*Kirkus Reviews*

"4/5* You're moving along at steady clip, completely immersed in Plotkin's journey and properly outraged by the irrational evidence that's stacked against him. Delightfully satirical, the author takes a jab at everything from judges, to juries, to lawyers, to public manipulation and ignorance, oftentimes with hilarious results." —*Manhattan Book Review*, Heather Clawson

JERE KRAKOFF was a civil rights attorney with the ACLU National Prison Project in Washington, D.C., the Lawyers Committee for Civil Rights Under Law in Mississippi, and a legal aid program in Pittsburgh. Website: jerekrakoff.com

Holistic Technology Integration: The P4 Framework for Professional Development ($15, 80pp, 6X9": Paperback ISBN: 978-1-68114-296-8; $30: Hardcover ISBN: 978-1-68114-297-5; $2.99: EBook ISBN: 978-1-68114-298-2; LCCN: 2016915594; January 17, 2017): The P4 Framework is a holistic framework for teacher technology use that discusses the use of technology to enhance instructional practices, teachers' professional development, and general workplace productivity. This framework shows the members of the teacher education field how to use technology not just for pedagogical practices, but also for the practical aspects of teaching. Conversely, it also illustrates the limits of the "tools-only" emphasis that is often promoted through technology conferences and social media.

This framework addresses complex issues regarding technology in education: teacher buy-in, balancing teacher and student needs, developing a professional development program that analyzes learners, the community, and teachers. The book is both an easy-to-read guide and a call-to-arms. It encourages school personnel to set benchmarks and track performance changes based on technology initiatives in order to prove to stakeholders that technology is indeed making a difference.

JASON SIKO is an Assistant Professor of Educational Technology at Grand Valley State University in Grand Rapids, MI. He was previously a high school biology and chemistry teacher for 13 years. Jason has also worked as a consultant in strategic foresight. His research interests include educator training and professional development, teaching foresight in K-12, game design as an instructional strategy, and K-12 online readiness skills.

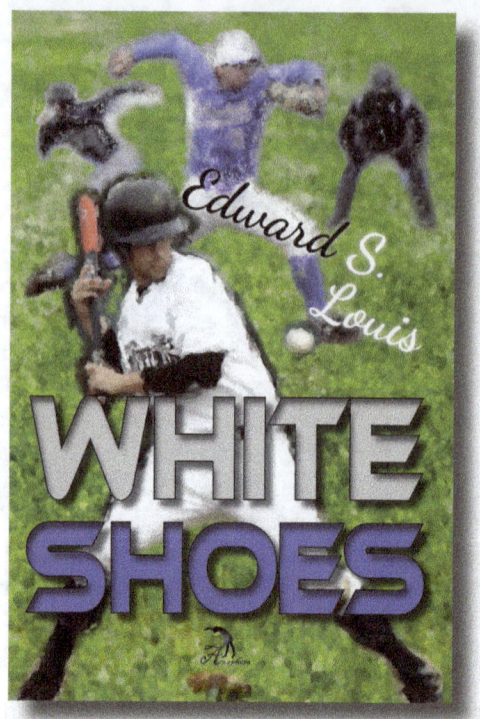

White Shoes: A Novel: ($20, 220pp, 6X9": Softcover ISBN-13: 978-1-68114-326-2; $35: Hardcover ISBN-13: 978-1-68114-327-9; $2.99: EBook ISBN-13: 978-1-68114-328-6; LCCN: 2017937215; Release: July 20, 2017): The adventures of young Willie Smith as he grows up in small-town America playing baseball and trying to learn what it means to "be a man." This novel engages the reader in the feel, sights, sounds, and smells of playing baseball: of playing the old game, not watching it on TV. Partly a comic coming-of-age story and even an apprenticeship novel, *White Shoes* shows the struggles of school, of growing up in a single-parent family, of emerging sexuality, and of trying to find one's place in the world, experiences both universal and individual to every human soul. From the first spring baseball of Willie's freshman year to graduation and hopes for something beyond the baseball diamond and the confines of Harmon Falls, a fading Midwestern coal and steel town, E. S. Louis brings people and town to life in an exploration of ways of life both past and yet still alive in more than memory, in how so many of us still experience the world. As a work of "Men's Studies," an offshoot of the increasingly popular field of Gender Studies, *White Shoes* asks essential questions about learning how to grow up to be a good man; as a work of postmodern fiction it treats narrative playfully and with humor.

EDWARD S. LOUIS' books include *Odysseus on the Rhine* (the story of Odysseus' adventures after he returns from Troy), *The Monster Specialist* (the story of Sir Severus le Brewse, knight of King Arthur's court, and the sorceress Lilava, his partner in love and adventure), *The Streets of Harmon Falls*, and the forthcoming *Wiskalo Chookalo*, a ghost story set in Depression-era Wisconsin. He lives in Wisconsin with his artist wife, Kristy, and his house lion, Bingley, and teaches literature and writing. Please see his short story "Little Fotungus" in the 2017 edition of *The Long Story*.

The Fajitas and Beer Convention: ($20, 152pp, 6X9", ISBN: 978-1-937536-94-7, $35: Hardcover ISBN: 978-1-68114-120-6, LCCN: 2014954338, October 2014): The story begins with the passing of little Manolo's mother. She left instructions with their ranch hand, Salvador, to deliver Manolo to their only family in the northern part of Mexico. Along the way, Manolo and Salvador encounter great adventures including a sinister drunk, a deceiving carnival owner, a magician, and the beautiful Paloma. The adventure does not end in northern Mexico! When Manolo and Salvador accidentally enter the United States on a train, they find themselves walking the streets of an American border town. Here they come across a wealthy neighborhood where ten Mexican gardeners are preparing to have a social. They explain that they all work for wealthy men, who are using the funds from their businesses to take vacations, meanwhile writing these off as, "conventions." So, every time their bosses leave, they use their houses to have their own "conventions" with fajitas and beer. Each of the men tells a tale during one of these socials, each with its own plot, moral lesson, and satire.

* Adopted as a supplementary material for 3 sections of ENGL 1301: Composition & Rhetoric I at the Lone Star College (TX)

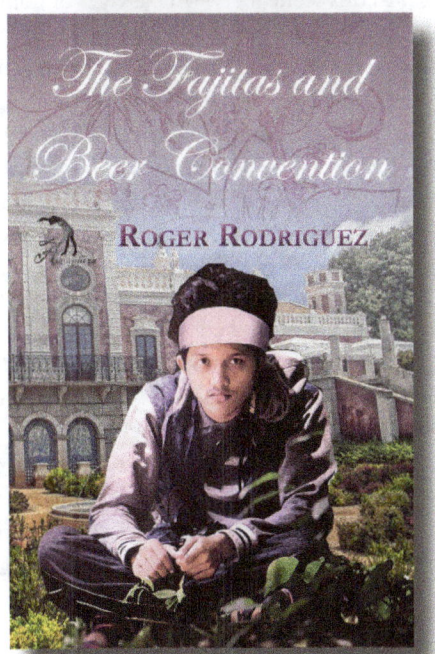

Six ($20: Paperback: ISBN-13: 978-1-68114-239-5; $35: Hardcover: 978-1-68114-240-1; $2.99: EBSCO EBook: ISBN-13: 978-1-68114-255-5; LCCN: 2016936296, 126pp, 6X9"; Release: April 18, 2016): "Roger Rodriguez's Six is a page turner to the highest degree. A cautionary tale of lust, obsession, and jealousy, where you can't help but look to see just how far down the rabbit hole goes for our protagonist, or if he'll ever be able to climb back out of those dark depths of the human psyche." —Dylan Herin-Soule, *Director/Producer*

"An amazing story driven by passion. Not your average love story." —*Actor*, Bobby Hernandez

"Not your typical romance. Excellent romantic thriller and a must read!" —*Journalist/News Anchor*, Ann Hutyra

When psychiatrist Duane Johnson reads his wife's diary, he learns the disturbing fact that during a short break-up, just prior to getting married, his wife Zulema had sex with six men. One would think that as a psychiatrist he would be able to manage the emotions involved in learning something like this, but his emotional condition spirals out of control./ Things get worse for him when his very sexy and voluptuous sister-in-law Julisa comes into the picture.

ROGER RODRIGUEZ is an American author born in Houston, Texas. He is a professor of Sociology at Texas A&M International University and of English and Sociology at Lone Star College. In 1998, Rodriguez won the Editor's Choice Award for outstanding poetry and the best paper in psychology at the 5th annual Guillermo Benavidez Academic Conference at Texas A&M International University. In 2008, Roger Rodriguez was featured on the Discovery Channel for his title "The Grass Beneath His Feet: The Charles Victor Thompson Story."

ARDOR: or How would-be Nobel Prize winner C. Milosz enjoyed the high life with low life in Italy, hobnobbed with a Viktor Yanukovych look-alike, and met his Muse on the rooftop of the Duomo ($20, 6X9", 130pp, Paperback ISBN-13: 978-1-68114-243-2, $35: Hardcover ISBN-13: 978-1-68114-244-9; $2.99: EBSCO EBook: 978-1-68114-254-8, LCCN: 2016904783, Release: August 1, 2016): "A political, social and intellectual satire, Ardor pokes fun at the overblown pretensions of professors, poets, journalists, policy-makers, businesspeople and foundation officers, and features none other than Viktor Yanukovych as one of its central characters." —*The Ukrainian Weekly*, "New Releases: Alexander Motyl's latest novel"

Chester Milosz, a very minor American poet who teaches at a very minor American college and aspires to win the Nobel, receives an invitation to a meeting of global high-flyers at the Otto Nabokov Foundation's Ardor Haus estate in Caravaggio, Italy. The organizers are Dickey Lemon, a British billionaire who made his fortune in hamster bedding, and Joe Zsasz, an ex-communist functionary-turned-international consultant. The participants are a sundry collection of business people, policymakers, journalists, and academics involved in shady dealings with a corrupt Eastern European president who closely resembles Ukraine's Viktor Yanukovych.

ALEXANDER **J. M**OTYL is a writer, painter, and professor. Nominated for the Pushcart Prize in 2008 and 2013, he is the author of seven novels. Motyl's artwork has been displayed in solo and group shows in New York, Philadelphia, and Toronto and is part of the permanent collection of the Ukrainian Museum in New York and the Ukrainian Cultural and Educational Centre in Winnipeg. He teaches at Rutgers University-Newark and is the author of six academic books, many articles, and a weekly blog on "Ukraine's Orange Blues."

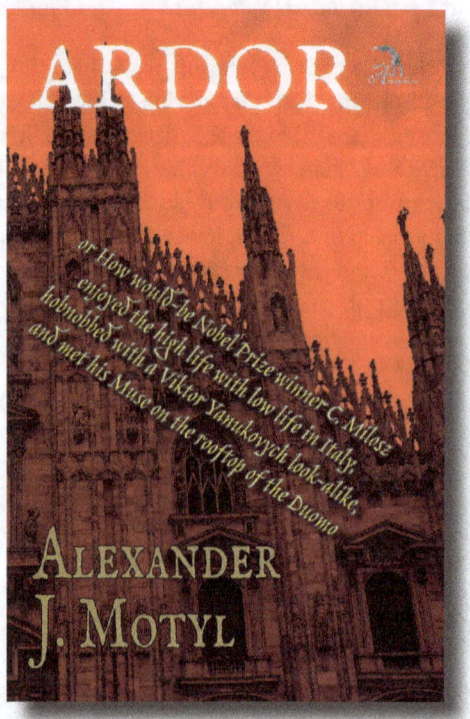

Global Warming: A Love Story ($20, 142pp, 6X9": Softcover ISBN-13: 978-1-68114-274-6; $35: Hardcover ISBN-13: 978-1-68114-275-3; $2.99: EBSCO EBook ISBN-13: 978-1-68114-276-0; LCCN: 2016941894; Release: July 1, 2016): a timeless love story, dressed up as treaties on climate change. A science teacher/aspiring writer, returns to school for professional development and falls head-over-heels for a "lithe and lovely" 20-year-old college student. Both are enrolled in a class that examines the nuances of global warming. They pass notes, flirt, and a relationship slowly evolves. But soon Julian, a hopeless romantic, discovers that Allison is due to marry her high school sweetheart. Julian risks all—including his job—to impress her, seduce her, and steal her away. During a final exam, he reads a treaty on the social economics of climate change. In this scene, between passages of political debate, are woven in a divine poem written centuries ago by Sappho. Allison is moved by his courtship and the real heartache begins. A romance, at the surface, but look closer at this hybrid and you'll find a deeply philosophical story addressing the fate of the planet and a workaholic-romantic who can't help but break his own heart. A fast-paced romance that will make women swoon and men laugh. At the very least, it will give women a gritty behind the scene look at their would-be seducers.

ANTONIO **J. H**OPSON writes poetry, speculative fiction, flash fiction, and essays. His work has appeared in The Harrow, SN-Review, Ascent Aspirations, Lost Magazine, The Piker Press, Akashic Books' Mondays Are Murder series, and NPR commentator Andrei Codrescu's Exquisite Corpse. He received Farmhouse Magazine's Reader's Choice Award and was invited to perform at Seattle's Richard Hugo House as a featured writer. He was selected to participate in Evergreen College's Literary Conference on "Activism and the Avant-Garde" and is a national EPPIE Award finalist. Website: Antoniohopson.com

An Englishman in Italian ($20: 978-1-68114-347-7; $35: Hardcover: 978-1-68114-348-4; $2.99: EBook: 978-1-68114-349-1; LCCN: 2017944017; Historical Fiction; Release: September 7, 2017): What if you woke up one day to find that you were famous? Lord Byron wrote that he woke up one day to find that he was famous. Centuries before, Will Shakespeare woke up to the dawning of his Shakespearean fame. An Englishman in Italian deals with the art of striving for success, the kind of success that leads to worldwide fame, and the perpetual longing for artistic immortality. But against the ambition of making it in the arts, the power of love and the force of death array themselves against the striving artists.

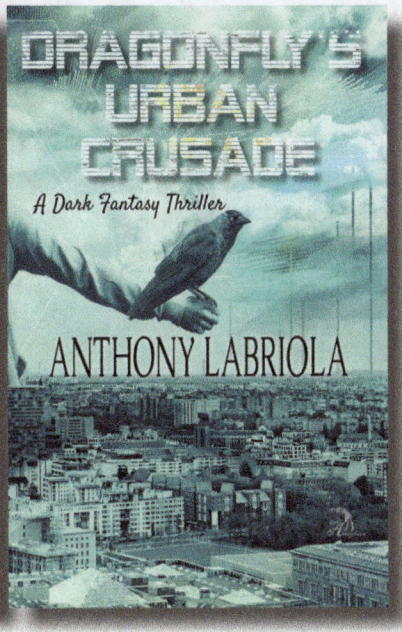

The Dandelion Clock: A Novel ($20: 978-1-68114-350-7; $35: Hardcover: 978-1-68114-351-4; $2.99: EBook: 978-1-68114-352-1; LCCN: 2017944014; September 2017): is a novel of resistance. In rage and fury, it is a protest against "the dying of the light." An old teacher, Leonardo Furioso, nicknamed Fury, sets out to delete his blighted memories of a life filled with misadventures, misdirected passion, and mistaken identity. The Dandelion Clock is also a portrait of a failed artist as an old man in a black frock coat with long, flaring, white hair. In his beleaguered and bewildered "second childishness" on the threshold of oblivion, Fury mocks both life and death as cruel jokes and joyous illusions, but delights in their cruel joy. The image of the dandelion clock refers to the childhood pastime of counting the puffs it takes to blow the seedhead off a dandelion in a past-flowering state to tell the time.

Dragonfly's Urban Crusade: A Dark Fantasy Thriller (Softcover: $20, 210pp, 6X9": ISBN-13: 978-1-68114-403-0; Hardcover: $35: ISBN-13: 978-1-68114-404-7; EBook: $2.99: ISBN-13: 978-1-68114-405-4;

LCCN: 2017916085; Fiction—Fantasy; Release: January 25, 2018): is a dark fantasy about the settling of old scores, and the longing for intimacy in a mysterious world. On his quest, a young man nicknamed Dragonfly sets out to solve the mystery of savage kidnappings, abductions, arson, and destruction in the Six. Fantasy and reality lead the detective and urban crusader to the discovery of a love greater than the one he once imagined.

Jealousy: Two Tales ($20, 128pp, 6X9": 978-1-68114-424-5; $35: Hardcover: 978-1-68114-425-2; $2.99: EBook: 978-1-68114-426-9; LCCN: 2018905252; Fiction—Short Stories; Release: October 20, 2018): "The Jealous Shoemaker" and "Numbered Days" are envy-tainted tales that deal with jealously guarded secrets of the past. The distant past has become a lost paradise for old men such as Pietro d'Arborio and Bliss (Dodo) Bane. Hell-bent on telling their versions of the truth, they also bear witness to life's stunning surprises, twisted ironies, dark enchantments, and puzzling mysteries. In a bewildering world, tainted by violence, guilt, jealousy, and revenge, they try to outface time's shocks, and get even with their tormentors and adversaries. Haunted, how can they prevail against past rejection, absurdity and horror? For these old men, is the past just baggage? Or is it never over? If they look for closure, will they be relieved to find it? The two tales in Jealousy link the shadows of the vanishing world with the realities of the here-and-now.

Anthony Labriola's work has appeared in *The Canadian Forum, PRISM international, Lo Straniero, Vallum: New International Poetics, Stone Voices,* and *Still Point Arts Quarterly, Passion: Poetry.* He studied at the University of Toronto and holds an M.A. in Drama. He taught English, Drama, and Performing Arts for thirty-two years. His other poetry collections include: *The Rigged Universe* (Shanti Arts) and *Sun Dogs* (Battered Suitcase Press). He teaches at Seneca College.

POETRY

Virgin Queen ($15, 92pp, 6X9", ISBN: 978-1-937536-98-5, $30: Hardcover ISBN: 978-1-68114-117-6, LCCN: 2014919876, December 2014): is a portrait of Queen Elizabeth I. Focusing on her interior life, it traverses her tragic love affairs and her fraught relationship with Mary, Queen of Scots, the cousin she never met. These pages illustrate her moments of defeat, her defiance, her strategies, her secrets, and her deathbed scene.

"Catherine Corman gives us an admirable companion in prose poems and photographs to one of England's greatest monarchs." —Lord Patten of Barnes, Chancellor of *The University of Oxford*

Catherine Corman's work has been exhibited in the Venice and Berlin Biennales. Her book of photographs, *Daylight Noir*, is in the collection of The Museum of Modern Art Library. She is the editor of *Joseph Cornell's Dreams*.

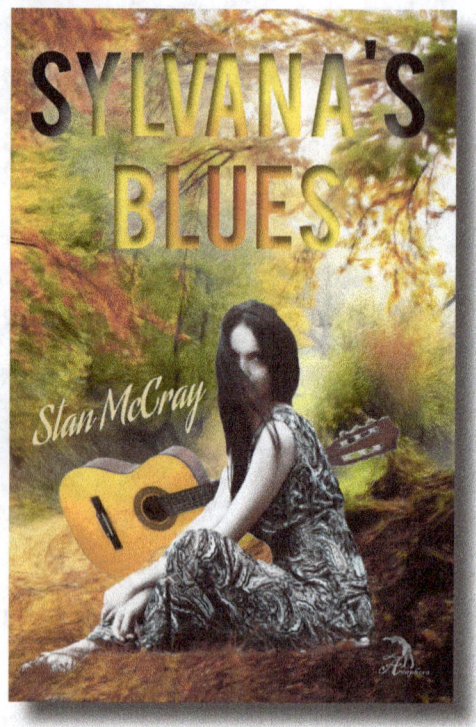

Sylvana's Blues ($15, 78pp, 6X9": Softcover: ISBN-13: 978-1-68114-344-6; $30: Hardcover: ISBN-13: 978-1-68114-345-3; $2.99: EBook: ISBN-13: 978-1-68114-346-0; LCCN: 2017908247; Edited by Nicholas Pagano; Poetry; Release: October 2, 2017): relates the story of a strange old man serving as an informal host to homeless individuals who come to partake of his stews and hear his music. He has largely given up on finding satisfaction in his lifelong search for some kind of fulfillment or self-discovery. Finally, he receives peace through what he learns during an unexpected visit from an even stranger young woman.

Stan McCray is an Associate Professor (Emeritus) of linguistics, French and intercultural communication at the University of Maryland, Baltimore County. He has been a blues guitarist and student of martial arts. He has long been interested in using modes of expression, found in various formal disciplines, to discover a Tao of aesthetics.

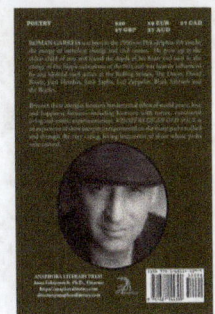

The Aqua Notebook (Softcover: $15: ISBN: 978-1-68114-466-5; Hardcover: $30: ISBN-13: 978-1-68114-467-2; EBook: $2.99: ISBN: 978-1-68114-468-9; LCCN: 2018954268; Poetry—American—General; Edited by: Salim Dharamshi; Release: February 20, 2019): is an invitation to discover poetry in the everyday experience. Following in the footsteps of David Lehman's *The Daily Mirror*, Frank O'Hara, and Emily Dickinson, this collection offers a poetic journal crafted out of life. Began in 2016 in an aqua notebook, this book of poetry chronicles one year. Locating the poetry and tiny moments of transcendence in our commonplace existence, Cotter crafts poetry from life, revealing the strange beauty that often exists in our daily lives. Approachable, conversational, and immediate, this collection offers poems that are at times spontaneous, but always carefully crafted. Locating moments of real joy and peace, Cotter illuminates our lives, asking us to look carefully for the poetic that's often in plain sight. She shows us how the smallest moments can elevate and inspire us. She writes, "Tonight I discovered what I discover / Each day: all along I wanted this / Exact miraculous thing."

Tasha Cotter is the author of the poetry collection *Some Churches* (Gold Wake Press, 2013) and the chapbooks *That Bird Your Heart* (Finishing Line Press, 2013) and *Girl in the Cave* (Tree Light Books, 2016). Winner of the 2015 Delphi Poetry Series, her work has appeared in journals such as *Contrary Magazine, NANO fiction*, and *Thrush*. A graduate of the University of Kentucky and the Bluegrass Writers Studio, she is included in the 2018-2019 Kentucky Humanities Speakers Bureau. A recipient of grants from the Kentucky Foundation for Women, The Kentucky Center, and the University of Kentucky Women's Forum, she makes her home in Lexington, Kentucky where she works in higher education and serves as the president-elect of the Kentucky State Poetry Society. You can find her online at http://www.tashacotter.com.

Whispers of an Old Soul (Softcover: $20, 298pp, 6X9": ISBN: 978-1-68114-439-9; Hardcover: $35: ISBN: 978-1-68114-440-5; Ebook: $2.99: ISBN: 978-1-68114-441-2; LCCN: 2018947762; Edited by: Elizabeth Coletti; Poetry—Subjects & Themes—Nature; Release: September 24, 2018): Between these energies Roman's fundamental ethos of world peace, love and happiness formed—including harmony with nature, communal living and artistic experimentation. *Whispers of an Old Soul* is an expression of these energies as experienced on the many paths walked and through the very caring, loving interaction of those whose paths were crossed.

Roman Garreis was born in the 1950's in Philadelphia, PA amidst the energy of turbulent change and civil unrest. He grew up as the oldest child of two and found the depth of his heart and soul in the energy of the hippie subculture of the 60's and was heavily influenced by and idolized such artists as the Rolling Stones, The Doors, David Bowie, Jimi Hendrix, Janis Joplin, Led Zeppelin, Black Sabbath and the Beatles.

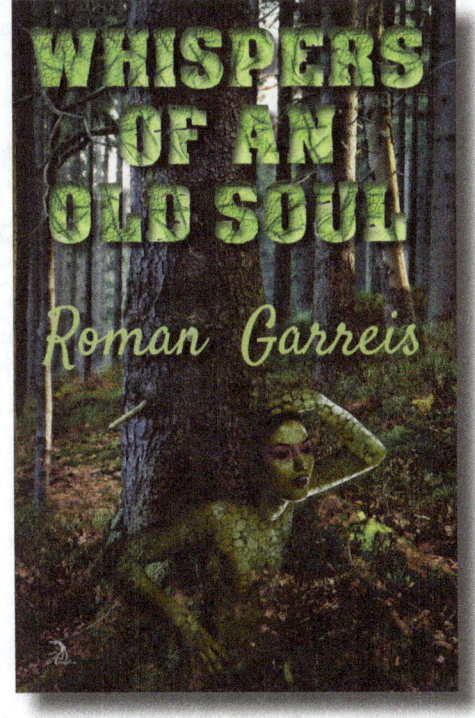

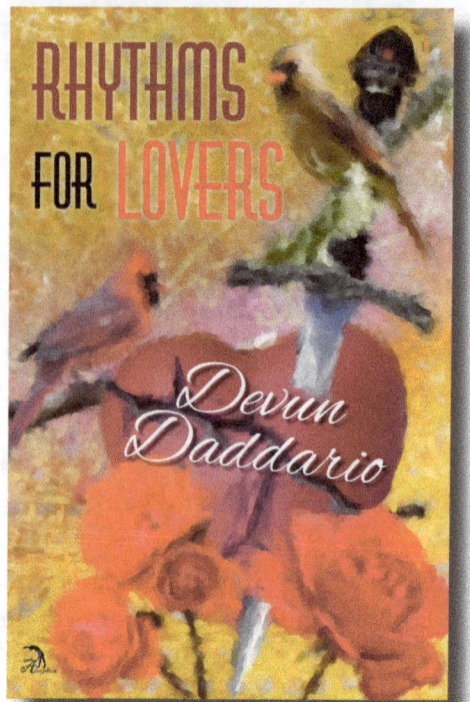

Rhythms for Lovers (Softcover: $15, 96pp, 6X9": 978-1-68114-412-2; Hardcover: $30: 978-1-68114-413-9; EBook: $2.99: 978-1-68114-414-6; LCCN: 2017919270; Edited by Ezra Koch; Poetry—Subjects & Themes—Love & Erotica; Release: March 25, 2018): a book of poems about the duality of Love. There is first, the love that is taught to us all. The idea of love that we are told exists, along with what we are exposed to and accumulate through years of sights and experiences. Then there is the love that can be learned. This is a love which grows only with perseverance and a continuous belief of knowing what is true to us until it blossoms into the rarest, purest love of unadulterated feelings defined by no specific parameters.

DEVUN DADDARIO was born and raised in Waco, Texas. He developed a deep interest for reading at an early age while his passion for writing grew from the literary influences of authors such as William Burroughs and Jack Kerouac along with the dialogue-driven films of writer/director Kevin Smith. He still resides in his hometown and in his spare time enjoys disc-golf, yoga and transcendental meditation.

Road Trip (Softcover: $15, 68pp, 6X9": ISBN: 978-1-68114-394-1; Hardcover: $30: ISBN-13: 978-1-68114-395-8; EBook: $2.99: ISBN-13: 978-1-68114-396-5; LCCN: 2017915102; Author's and Cover Photos by Will Hanley III; Poetry—Subjects & Themes—Death, Grief, Loss; Release: October 1, 2017): Mary Stone Hanley's debut collection of poems, a journey at the same time physical, historical, and spiritual. While it travels through the realms of childhood and approaching death, it also plots the way along the road from Civil Rights, to the Black Arts Movement, to avant-garde jazz of the 1960s, and the Black Lives Matter movement of contemporary times. In a stirring section essential to the message of her poetry, the author "translates" John Coltrane's *Love Supreme* into verse, culminating with a resounding "Thank you, God," spoken in unison by the jazz great and the poet herself. As her passing approaches, the speaker of these poems doesn't flinch at endings: but her affirmations move like her poetry toward openings and possibility. "No matter how the dream may go," she writes in the final poem, "Dialectically Speaking," "there is no end/ no last." *Road Trip* is a journey that disappears into the vanishing point, recognizing along the way that past, future and even existence itself is defined by who is looking and what one chooses to acknowledge. With a clear eye and with the poise and cadence of a master, Mary Stone Hanley guides us to the trail's end, where witness and compassion become the measure of a life.

MARY STONE HANLEY, Ph.D. was a playwright, poet, educator, scholar and researcher. As a playwright, she wrote nine plays for young people and two screenplays produced as films. She wrote and produced "The Name Game" in the 2013 DC Black Theater Festival and a revised version in the 2014 Capital Fringe Festival facilitated by grants from the D.C. Arts and Humanities Commission. She has a Ph.D. in Drama from the University of Washington and an MFA from American University.

Notes for Further Research (Softcover: $15, 62pp, 6X9”: ISBN: 978-1-68114-388-0; Hardcover: $30: ISBN: 978-1-68114-389-7; EBook: $2.99: ISBN: 978-1-68114-390-3; LCCN: 2017954772; Poetry—Women Authors; Release: December 15, 2017): is a step back (in terms of certainty) from Kirschner’s first book Hard Proof. It explores atheism, God, and free will with equal parts of humor, sincerity, and sensory delight.

MOLLY KIRSCHNER is a poet, playwright and graduate of Bennington College. Her first book of poems was *Hard Proof* (Red Mountain Press, 2015). Kirschner’s poems have appeared in numerous journals, as well as in Italian translation. Her new play *L’appel du Vide* premiered in July of 2017 in New York City.

“Molly Kirschner’s poems are loaded with dazzling imagery, originality of expression, and a sure sense of timing. Her abiding attention to the scientific facts of the natural world coalesces with an associative, unpredictable, and exhilarating sensibility to invent a language all its own.” –Akiko Busch, author of *The Incidental Steward*

Book Trailer: https://youtu.be/dt-Spy_dcJ8

Blue Mat: Poems After Yang Wanli (Softcover: $15: ISBN-13: 978-1-68114-397-2; Hardcover: $30: ISBN-13: 978-1-68114-398-9; EBook: $2.99: ISBN-13: 978-1-68114-399-6; LCCN: 2017915768; Edited by Mitchell Postich; Poetry—Canadian; Release: January 15, 2018): These poems are written in the spirit of Yang Wanli, one of the four major poets of the Southern Song Dynasty in China. Each poem touches on the miraculous detail of everyday experience, following Yang Wanli’s iconoclastic attention to the ordinary, in keeping with his practice of Chan Buddhism. In addition to the translations, adaptations and original poems inspired by Yang Wanli, there are also a number of translations of poems by the late Tang Dynasty poet Du Mu.

“Arthur Bull’s mantra, meditation and musing all poetic feels exactly like that of his long departed Chinese partners in crime. Except they contain some of the scraps and flotsam and jetsam of our so called modern world. Bull does capture, very succinctly, our slow march against time and circumstance. It’s all done carefully as mice and with admirable brevity… Arthur Bull has done a remarkable thing with *Blue Mat, Poems After Yang Wanli*. Bull has brought two Chinese poets, long part of the ether, back to life and respected them with his beautiful homage. We should all be so kind to our heroes. *Blue Mat, Poem After Yang Wanli* was nothing but pleasure. Arthur Bull writes the simple line, with the weight of the world hovering.”
—*Today’s Book of Poetry*, Michael Dennis, April 29, 2018

ARTHUR BULL lives in Nova Scotia, Canada. He has previously published three books of poetry, as well as four chapbooks. His poems and translations from classical Chinese have appeared in numerous Canadian and international journals. Bull is also a musician, and has worked for a number of small-scale fishery organizations.

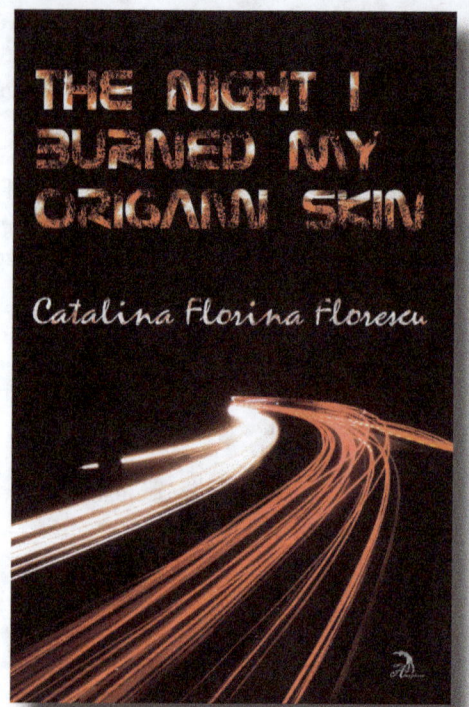

The Night I Burned My Origami Skin (Softcover: $15, 54pp, 6X9": ISBN: 978-1-68114-385-9; Hardcover: $30: ISBN: 978-1-68114-386-6; EBook: $2.99: ISBN: 978-1-68114-387-3; LCCN: 2017954204; Edited by Mallory Cormack; American Poetry; Release: December 15, 2017): The poems comprised in this collection address issues related to loss, longing, desire, on the one hand, and social justice, inequality, and language, on the other hand. I have returned to poetry because I felt that only through this genre I may be able to transfer my latent feelings, push them outside of me. Writing poetry has made me reconnect with my own homo ludens, yet paradoxically I am now more fragmented and slippery than ever, a kaleidoscope ready to be deposited in my readers' hands.

Florina Florescu was born in Romania. She earned her Bachelor's Degree from University of Bucharest. She holds a Master's Degree and a PhD in Comparative Literature from Purdue University. She teaches literature and writing at Pace University. Her books are in permanent libraries worldwide as well as at the Library of Congress in Washington, D.C. She is the author of: *Transacting Sites of the Liminal Bodily Spaces; Disjointed Perspectives on Motherhood; Inventing Me/Exerciții de retrăit.* Her next edited book, *Transnational Narratives of Englishes in Exile,* will be released in November 2017, and it will be exhibited at the MLA convention, followed by a book launch organized by CEERES of Voices affiliated with University of Chicago. Her political parable, *Suicidal Dog & Laika,* will have a table reading at The Immigrants' Theatre Project in New York City. With Mia, a drama, she will have a reading at the Romanian Cultural Institute in New York. She delivered papers at Harvard, Sorbonne, New York University. Her Scrabble Cancer Poster was presented at the Museum of Modern Art in NYC and at Boston University. Her next goal is to see her plays performed. She is also working on a collection of short/flash stories titled *Not Yet.*

A Mural by the Sea: Poems ($15: Softcover: ISBN-13: 978-1-68114-341-5; $30: Hardcover: ISBN-13: 978-1-68114-342-2; $2.99: EBook: ISBN-13: 978-1-68114-343-9; LCCN: 2017942418; Edited by: Laura McCarthy; Poetry—Caribbean & Latin American; Release: October 15, 2017): Poetry and masquerade have always resided in me. I know them to be inspired, and when well rendered, magical. From San Fernando to Brooklyn, poetry is the Carnival, and the Trinidad Carnival finds its way into my poetry—as visual and oral experience—everyday living, a painted face J'ouvert morning. Many of the poems in this volume have aged with me and over that time, and again like my own life, been transformed into some measure of sustained lucidity. The heart of these poems speaks to ordinary men and women and the world about them. From this landscape, language and experience comes *A Mural by the Sea.*

After living and working in Brooklyn for nearly four decades as a poet, journalist/editor and artist, **Dawad Philip** has since re-settled in his hometown of San Fernando, Trinidad. The author of Invocations (1980), Philip's poems have appeared in several anthologies including *Steppingstones, Bomb, Caribbean Voices* and most recently, *past simple*. A 1990 recipient of New York State Fellowship on the Arts (Poetry), Philip was one of five poets selected to represent Brooklyn in a Brooklyn-Leningrad Literary Exchange in the 1990s. He has performed his works in the Caribbean, U.S., Canada; Riga, Latvia; Moscow and St. Petersburg, and selected poems have been translated into Russian by the former Leningrad Writers Union. Philip, who holds a Masters of Arts (Carnival Arts) degree from the University of Trinidad and Tobago, keeps an active hand in the annual Trinidad Carnival and further afield as a costume designer and mask-maker.

"A brilliant work infused with an imagery." —*Geoffrey Dunn*

Light's Battered Edge: Poems: ($15, 96pp, 6X9", Print ISBN: 978-1-68114-217-3, EBook ISBN: 978-1-68114-218-0, LCCN: 2015917029, November 2015): "Catches sight of 'a sparrow by its own forgotten self,' and that sparrow stands in for other 'forgotten' ones: the homeless, the wrecked, the ill, a family of forebears 'visited' by comprehensive Job-like 'Misery.' These compelling poems leave us disquieted, as much by beauty as by sorrow." —Nathalie F. Anderson, Professor, Swarthmore College

"Think of the spirit of place as the frame of memory shaping language, of the perpetual soliloquy of being who you are in counterpoint with echoing phrases others have uttered at or to you, and you will have some idea of the chant and enchantment of the poems gathered in Light's Battered Edge. There are some hard truths in these poems—about abusive spouses, about the wear and tear of caring for others. But underlying it all is the sense of what love really means." —Frank Wilson, *Books, Inq.; The Epilogue*

"She is now making her mark as a poet." –Justine Heinze, *Roxborough-Manayunk Patch*

DIANE SAHMS-GUARNIERI is the author of two full-length poetry collections: *Images of Being* (Stone Garden Publishing) and *Night Sweat* (Red Dashboard Press). She has been published in *The Philadelphia Inquirer, Pennsylvania Literary Journal, Many Mountains Moving, Philadelphia Stories, Blue Collar Review,* and *Wilderness House Literary Review*, among others. Awarded a grant in poetry from the AEV Foundation in 2013, she is the 2015 "Winner" of Partisan Press's "Working People's Poetry Competition." She currently serves as Poet in Residence at Ryerss Museum and Library and as Poetry Editor of the *Fox Chase Review*. More info about Guarnieri: dianesahms-guarnieri.com

Birds on Elephant ($15, 6X9", 70pp, ISBN: 978-1-68114-002-5, $30: Hardcover ISBN: 978-1-68114-111-4, LCCN: 2014959352, January 2015): all of the landscape is an allusion, and "we borrow or skim on [it], and our work becomes more fertile." Each poem in the collection either perches on a great work or a famed poet, or has first words that make a sentence if read downward—as in:

Across and Down

Frame your memory so I could see it tomorrow.
Your place in mine has gone off with the tide.
Memory is not quite the warmth that was once on me.
So gather the particles and weigh in; it's not too dispersed.
I will look up and fly the gossamer of you yesterday.
Could you withstand the mind without the frame?
See it against the sea.
It will elevate with the sun. I'll just diminish
tomorrow.

TED BERNAL GUEVARA divides his eagerness, his out-of-bed thrill, into two compartments: Fiction, a rustic room where things are arranged and accessible with a calendar tacked on the wall above his head, and Poetry, the balcony attached to that room. He hardly urges himself to stand up and walk out. He just does, and the air out there is profoundly fresh. Guevara is the author of *Films*, a book of 55 poems based on 55 movies, and three novels, *A Circle with Two Corners, Days of Slint*, and *True Feel*. He resides in Speedway, Indiana.

The Sleep of Reason Produces Monsters: (Softcover: $25, 170pp, 6X9": ISBN: 978-1-68114-356-9; Hardcover: $40: ISBN-13: 978-1-68114-357-6; Release: December 19, 2017): The poems were written in the poet's youth at the beginning of his experiments and poetic explorations. With sheer lyrical madness, poets such as Dante Alighieri, William Shakespeare, Charles Baudelaire, Paul Verlaine, T S Eliot, Ezra Pound, WB Yeats, Samuel Beckett, Dylan Thomas, Anthony Burgess, Thomas Merton, Eugenio Montale and Leonard Cohen haunt the poet's inner life in *The Sleep of Reason Produces Monsters*. They are often approximations of earlier works, translations or transliterations of dead poets. At other times, in daring homage or tribute, the poems *interrogate* each other, or interact and strive to get at their hidden truths. Some of the pieces, in different forms, have appeared in various magazines and collections.

Armour & Lace ($20, 126pp, 6X9": Softcover: ISBN: 978-1-68114-358-3; $35: Hardcover: ISBN-13: 978-1-68114-359-0; $2.99: EBook: ISBN-13: 978-1-68114-360-6; Poetry—Subjects & Themes—Love & Erotica; Release: December 1, 2017): deals with desire, its myths and ever-evolving realities. The free-form poems trace the arc of a journey on which there are joys and sorrows, a sense of delight, and the re-configuring of lives lived. Beyond bewilderment and mystification, the poems also converse with grief and wonder. These poems yearn for the perfect arrow that will hit the target of understanding. They seek the mysteries of self-surrendering love, and reveal the fragmentation of visions of love. Though we are wounded in battle, we continue in our quests to know ourselves through experiences in the real world.

This Mortal Earth: A Year of Beginnings and Ceasings: ($15, 114pp, 6X9", ISBN: 978-1-68114-008-7, $30: Hardcover ISBN: 978-1-68114-109-1, LCCN: 2015930077, January 2015): The poems in this collection were written one-a-day, during the course of the author's sixty-seventh year. They seek to express an ecological awareness, the "intense consciousness of land" (Aldo Leopold), a consciousness of the Earth's land and of that essence that composes the writer's being.

FRED WAAGE is Professor of Literature and Language at East Tennessee State University. He was raised in upstate New York, got his academic degrees from Princeton, and taught in many U.S. states including California, Illinois, and Pennsylvania. He has had many nonacademic jobs including Research Associate at the Huntington Library and Assistant Manager at Jack-in-the-Box. He also published chapbooks, poetry, and fiction. His most recent book is *Sinking Creek Journal: An Environmental Book of Days*.

ANTHONY LABRIOLA'S work has appeared in *The Canadian Forum, PRISM international, Lo Straniero, Vallum: New International Poetics, Stone Voices,* and *Still Point Arts Quarterly, Passion: Poetry.* He studied at the University of Toronto and holds an M.A. in Drama. He taught English, Drama, and Performing Arts for thirty-two years. His other poetry collections include: *The Rigged Universe* (Shanti Arts) and *Sun Dogs* (Battered Suitcase Press). Anaphora Literary Press has published his prose works: *Devouring the Artist, The Pros & Cons of Dragon-Slaying,* and *Poor Love & Other Stories.* He teaches at Seneca College.

Voices Against Silence: ($15, ISBN: 978-1-937536-86-2, $30: Hardcover ISBN: 978-1-68114-124-4, 6X9", 98pp): employs a variety of tones, ranging from the deadly serious to the humorous, as, celebrating language, it addresses materials drawn from both the human and natural worlds. In accordance with this, it stands ready, at one moment, to contemplate a pet cat, at another, the cosmos.

ALAN HOLDER was born and bred in Brooklyn, and then received his A.B., M.A. and Ph.D from Columbia University. Over a period of forty years he taught at Columbia College, University of Vermont, University of Southern California, Williams, and Cornell, but principally at Hunter College of the City University of New York. He has published four books and several articles in the field of literary criticism. For two years after retiring, he wrote a weekly column on the environment for *The Redding Pilot*. He also served as a teacher's assistant in day-care centers. Having specialized in the teaching of poetry during his career, he continues to teach it at The Ridgefield Public Library. His poems have appeared in a variety of venues, and he is the author of two chapbooks of verse, *Opened: A Mourning Sequence* and *Aging Heard in the Clouds*.

Sky Gazer: ($20, 142pp, 6X9", Print ISBN: 978-1-68114-207-4, EBook ISBN: 978-1-68114-208-1, LCCN: 2015915803, April 2016): Firmly rejecting the unabashed subjectivity and accompanying impenetrability of much contemporary verse , Alan Holder's *Sky Gazer,* from first to last, makes its poems steadily available to the reader, assumed to be "a creature of feeling" and addressed directly. The reader is onboard for a train ride or in-step for a woodland walk. It continually registers that great commonality of human experience, the four seasons. The poems share the sights that come the poet's way—so much of what he sees assumes the status of spectacle—the source of many of those arresting sights being the heavens, which Holder never tires of contemplating. He has a fondness for long, winding verse sentences; some poems consist of but a single one. Again and again, Holder alludes, sometimes implicitly, to works by great figures of the literary past—Shakespeare, Milton, Wordsworth, Tennyson, Melville, Twain, Yeats, Frost, Stevens, Eliot, Dylan Thomas—using them as springboards to go his own way. Repeatedly, his poems raise questions that do not admit of answers. *Sky Gazer* takes seriously one of the prescriptions for poetry that Stevens sets forth in Notes toward a *Supreme Fiction*: "It Must Give Pleasure."

"Whether addressing vegetarianism, the natural world, or the experience of jogging, Holder's poems are invitations to enjoy, think, and discuss. This accessible collection of poems, replete with cultural references, is an excellent choice for poetry workshops for teens and a stimulating choice for book-talks." —Hilary Crew, February 2015, *VOYA Magazine*

Mind and Body: And Other Stories: ($20, 130pp, 6X9", ISBN-13: 978-1-68114-233-3, February 2016): is a subtly linked series of stories that chronicle two generations of a family from the Depression to World War II to the Vietnam War to the present. Characters include a jazz trumpeter, a Ukrainian teenager taken by the Nazis for slave labor in Germany, soldiers from World War II and the Vietnam War, and a strange crew of college professors and their wives from a small college in the Midwest.

LUCAS CARPENTER was born in Elberton, Georgia. He was educated at the College of Charleston (B.S.), the University of North Carolina at Chapel Hill (M.A.), and the State University of New York at Stony Brook (Ph.D.). He is the author of *John Gould Fletcher and Southern Modernism* (U. of Arkansas Press, 1990) and general editor of a seven-volume series devoted to Fletcher's work. He has also written a chapbook of poetry, *A Year for the Spider* (UNC Pitcher Poetry Award, 1973), and a book of poetry, *Perils of the Affect* (Mellen Press, 2002). His poems, stories, articles and reviews have appeared in thirty-seven periodicals, including *Prairie Schooner, The Minnesota Review, Beloit Poetry Journal, College Literature, Kansas Quarterly, Carolina Quarterly, Concerning Poetry, Poetry* (Australia), *Southern Humanities Review, College English, San Francisco Review of Books, Callaloo, Chronicle of Higher Education*, and *New York Newsday*. He was awarded a Fulbright fellowship to lecture and write in Belgium during the 1999-2000 academic year. He is Charles Howard Candler Professor of English at Oxford College, Emory University.

Glurk! A Hellbender Odyssey: ($20, 160pp, 6X9", ISBN-13: 978-1-68114-231-9, 22 photographs, January 2016): is the first book-length, epic poem about Cryptobranchus alleganiensis, aka North America's largest salamander. Through an investigative poetic lens of folklore, history, science and ecology, grotesque-advocate Mark Spitzer paints a four-part profile of an amazing phenomenon. This semi-monstrous mosaic of a living, breathing barometer of water quality and biodiversity is accomplished through a visionary voice that incorporates research, data, primary sources, and images that twist and torque like an actual bender (as the mythology goes) wending its way back to hell.

MARK SPITZER is the author of twenty-three books, including fish books, novels, memoirs, collections of poetry, and literary translation. He is currently an associate professor of creative writing at the University of Central Arkansas, and the Editor in Chief of the award-winning literary journal, *Toad Suck Review* (toadsuckreview.org). For more information on Spitzer, take a look at sptzr.net.

"The poems range from scientific narratives to neologism-filled lyrics, connecting us to our own wildness, playing on our own youthful enthusiasms, humor and curiosity. Most importantly, the poet suggests that imagination begins the solution to even the most serious problem, even the threat of extinction." —Lea Graham, author of *This End of the World: Notes to Robert Kroetsch* (Apt. 9 Press, 2016)

"Mark Spitzer really captured the hellbender story here in an informative and entertaining manner. The presentation is digestible (not technical) and creative… This is a great way to reach a broad audience and convey the plight of this amphibian." —Dr. Donald Shepard, Amphibian Biologist, University of Louisiana, Monroe

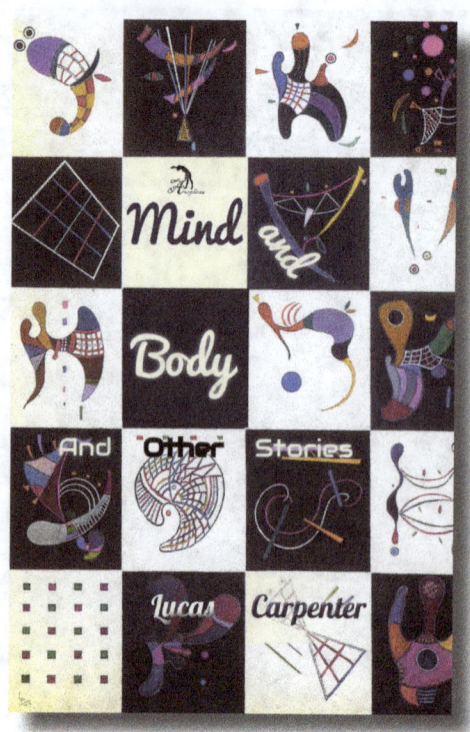

Trucker Dude: Confessions of a Ramblin' Man ($20, 164pp, 6X9": Paperback: ISBN-13: 978-1-68114-277-7; $35: Hardback: ISBN-13: 978-1-68114-278-4; $2.99: EBook ISBN-13: 978-1-68114-279-1; LCCN: 2016942467; August 1, 2016): TD is an artist and former football player who has a sore ass from long-haul trucking. He's thinking about taking a year off just to paint and hang out with his girlfriend, Linda Sue, when his trucker friend Flynn proposes an armored car heist. TD—short for Tommy Dennison and Trucker Dude—agrees to go along with the elaborate plan, despite serious misgivings. He quits his trucking job, but not before a final run from Seattle to Miami. On the road he meets Jason, a hitchhiking singer-songwriter with hippie and religious tendencies. Jason was studying for the priesthood, but his sideline as a chick magnet derailed that career course. As they gradually become friends, TD confides his qualms about the heist. He also has qualms about marriage, but Linda Sue is getting tired of her girlfriend status, giving TD a lot to think about out there on the highway of life.

Spotlight on Alaska Books: *Trucker Dude*, July 28, 2016

John **F**oley is a writer, teacher and artist living in Prescott Valley, Arizona. John has written several YA novels, including *Hoops of Steel*, which was named a Book for the Teen-Age in 2008. In addition, he has been Artist-in-Residence at several national parks, and his paintings have been juried into many shows. Currently John works as a high school English teacher. He is a former newspaper reporter, and his freelance work has appeared in *Sail Magazine, Alaska Magazine, Heinemann Books for Young Readers* and many other publications.

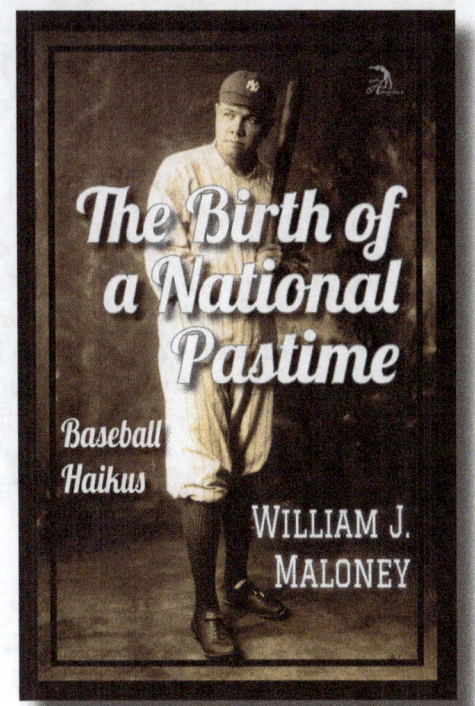

The Birth of a National Pastime: Baseball Haikus: ($15, 64pp, 6X9", 48 Photographs, LCCN: 2016906912; Paperback ISBN-13: 978-1-68114-265-4; $30: Hardcover ISBN-13: 978-1-68114-266-1; E-Book ISBN-13: 978-1-68114-267-8; Release: May 25, 2016): This collection of poems is a humorous and insightful glimpse into the lives of fifty early pioneers of the game of baseball. The subjects of this collection include players, executives and other contributors to the game which we now refer to as a national pastime.

Dr. **W**illiam **J**. **M**aloney is a clinical associate professor at New York University College of Dentistry. He is a fellow of the Academy of Dentistry International, the New York Academy of Medicine, the Royal Society of Medicine and the Pierre Fauchard Academy. Dr. Maloney is the author of over 270 professional publications. He has also been presented with the Award of Excellence from The Floating Hospital of New York City. He has also been inducted into various prestigious organizations and societies, such as The New York Academy of Medicine and The Royal Society of Medicine.

SHORT STORIES

Dangerous Obsessions ($15, ISBN: 978-1-937536-16-9, $30: Hardcover ISBN: 978-1-68114-107-7, LCCN: 2011945742, PS3610.A735 H68 2011, 6X9", 106pp, January 28, 2012): **2015 Books of the Year! Short Fiction**: "Of the dozen stand-out individual short story collections I enjoyed in 2015, Van Laerhoven's was the standy-outiest. [His] stories always surprise without descending into the cheap thrills of fakery and he uses his journalistic experience to write about the cold and the cruel aspects of human nature with unflinching truth." —Hubert O'Hearn, *San Diego Book Review*

"A philosophical exploration of the human condition, a confrontation with the darkest corners of our minds. I highly recommend this moving and gripping collection of stories to anyone seeking to be moved by something truly thought-provoking." —*Quick Book Reviews*, David Ben Efraim

"Recommend it to anyone who likes short, dramatic & down to the earth crime/mystery stories 4/4*" —*OnlineBookClub*

BOB VAN LAERHOVEN: a fulltime Belgian/Flemish author, Laerhoven published more than 30 books in Holland, Belgium and the US. Three-time finalist of the **Hercule Poirot Prize** for best mystery novel of the year with the novels *Djinn* and *The Finger of God*. Winner of the Hercule Poirot Prize for *Baudelaire's Revenge,* which also won the **USA Best Book Award 2014** in the category "mystery/suspense". His last novel, *De schaduw van de Mol* is currently being translated into English as *The Shadow of the Mole.*

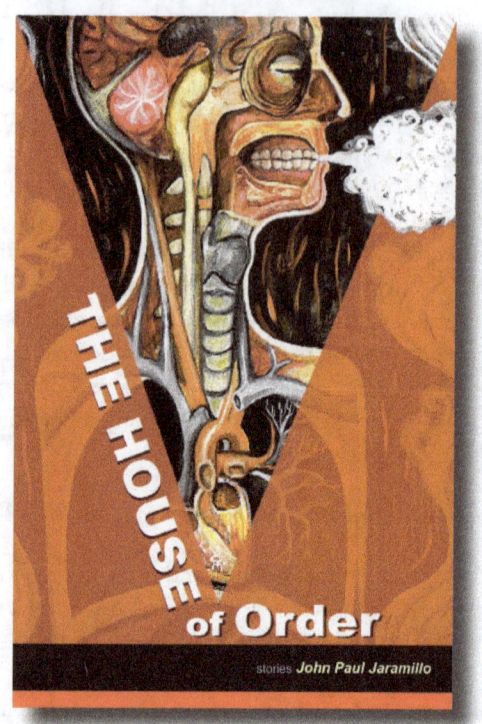

#6 on the 2013 Top 10 New Latino Authors to Watch (and Read) List

Finalist for Latino Literacy Now's Mariposa Award Best First Fiction Book Award

The House of Order ($15, ISBN: 978-1-937536-16-9, $30: Hardback ISBN: 978-1-68114-170-1, LCCN: 2011945742, PS3610.A735 H68 2011, 6X9", 106pp, January 2012): the first collection of composite stories by John Paul Jaramillo, presents a stark vision of American childhood and family. Set in Southern Colorado and Northern New Mexico, Manito's only access to his lost family's story is his uncle, the unreliable Neto Ortiz. Manito sorts family truth from legend as broken as the steel industry and the rusting vehicles that line Spruce Street.

"Raw and highly emotional at times, Jaramillo's stories give a realistic look in to the lives of his characters as he presents short vignettes that hint at a deeper family saga. His style is easy to read and his concise wording retains a surprising amount of detail. A compelling set of stories" —*San Francisco Book Review*

JOHN PAUL JARAMILLO grew up in Southern Colorado but now lives, writes and teaches in Springfield, Illinois. He earned his MFA in creative writing (fiction) from Oregon State University and, currently, holds the position of Associate Professor of English in the Arts and Humanities Department of Lincoln Land Community College.

PENNSYLVANIA LITERARY JOURNAL

ISSN 2151-3066 (print)
EDITOR: ANNA FAKTOROVICH

PENNSYLVANIA LITERARY JOURNAL (Catalog #: PN80 .P46) is a printed peer-reviewed journal that publishes critical essays, book-reviews, short stories, interviews, photographs, art, and poetry. PLJ is available through the EBSCO Academic Complete and ProQuest databases in full-text. It is also on sale as single issues on Amazon, Barnes and Noble and most other online bookstores. It is listed in the MLA International Bibliography, the MLA Directory of Periodicals, Genamics JournalSeek, and Duotrope's Digest. The journal is a member of the Council of Literary Magazines and Presses. PLJ has published works by and interviews with established journal editors, Sundance Film Festival and Brooklyn Film Festival winners, and best-selling authors and scholars.

CINEMATIC CODES REVIEW features works in all visual genres, especially those with moving pictures, be they music videos, feature films, documentaries, photography, or just about any other mode or genre of art that does not fall into the realm of "literature." The other term in the name is "codes" and the intention here is to go beyond the simple summary or theme of the projects criticized in this journal's pages to the codes and meanings that are hidden beyond the superficial.

"Thank you for a very fair review of my show. You seem to understand it very well. Appreciate you taking the time to go through several episodes, not just the pilot. Many more good things on the way and hopefully the show will get even better. I'm certainly having a blast." —Jack Maxwell, Host, *Booze Traveler*, **Travel Channel**

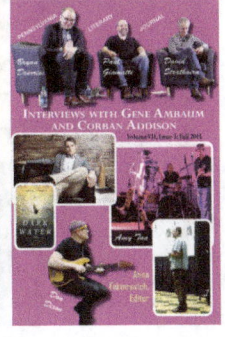

CINEMATIC CODES REVIEW

ISSN 2473-3385 (print)/2473-3377 (online)

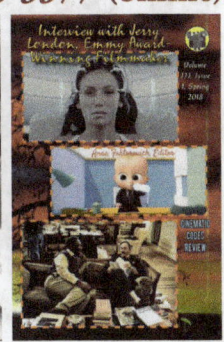

Interviews with Geraldine Brooks and Farmers: Volume VII, Issue 1: ($15, 166pp, 7X10", Spring 2015, 84 photographs, ISBN: 978-1-512068-34-4): This issue begins with an interview with the Pulitzer Prize winning author, Geraldine Brooks, who talks about the writing craft, her novels and her life outside of fiction. This feature is followed by four interviews with farmers from the Frankfort, Kentucky region, one of whom, Michael Spencer, is on the Kentucky state Farm Bureau board and another, Richard Jones, runs the regionally well-known Happy Jack's Pumpkin Farm.

Interviews with Best-Selling Young Adult Writers: Volume IV, Issue 3 ($10, Fall 2012, ISBN-13: 978-1-937536-38-1, $30: Hardback ISBN: 978-1-68114-156-5, 6X9", 112pp): Interviews with Cinda Williams Chima, James Dashner and Carrie Ryan, all New York Times best-selling young adult fiction writers. They are interviewed by Catherine W. Griffin, who has a Master's of Science in Journalism from Columbia University. They share their experiences with writing in a popular genre, and give specific advice for both new and professional writers.

Interviews with Gene Ambaum and Corban Addison: Volume VII, Issue 3, Fall 2015: ($20, 214pp, 6X9", ISBN: 978-1-519787-95-8, 40+ photographs): This issue includes an interview with Gene Ambaum, one of the creators of the popular *Unshelved* cartoon about a library. The second featured interview is with Corban Addison, the author of three international bestselling novels, *A Walk Across the Sun*, *The Garden of Burning Sand*, and *The Tears of Dark Water*.

Interviews with Novelists: Volume VI, Issue 2: ($10, 178pp, 6X9", Summer 2014, ISBN: 978-1-937536-84-8): Features interviews with best-selling and award winning novelists. Bob Van Laerhoven, winner of the 2007 Knack Hercule Poirot Prize, for his mystery novel, *Baudelaire's Revenge*, talks about his horses, literary fiction, and about the boundaries of obscenity. John Michael Cummings, winner of The Paterson Prize for Books for Young People for his novel, *The Night Freed John Brown*, discusses reasons for writing young adult fiction, selling the first novel to Penguin, and other curious topics. Bestselling visionary author of *The Transhumanist Wager*, Zoltan Istvan, chats about the adventures he had working for *National Geographic*, and his philosophy.

 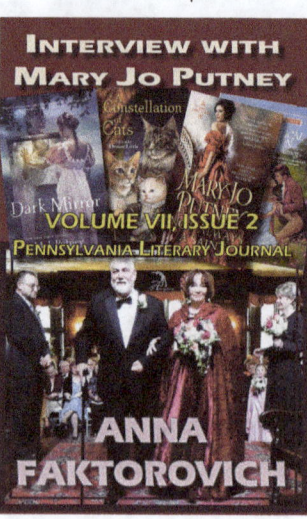  

INTERVIEW WITH LARRY NIVEN: VOLUME V, ISSUE 2 ($10, 6X9", SUMMER 2013, 68PP, ISBN: 978-1-937536-49-7): This special issue of the Pennsylvania Literary Journal: Interview with Larry Niven features an interview with the best-selling science fiction author, Larry Niven, in which he discusses the writing craft, the life of a professional writer, and his unique science fiction style. Niven's Ringworld has won many prestigious international awards, and his newly released collection of short stories, The Draco Tavern is one of the best recent examples of structured, literary science fiction. The issue also includes a short story from the editor, Anna Faktorovich, "Coal and Rice" about a struggling Chinese rice farmer and a wealthy, corrupt Chinese businessman. Kehinde Wiley, a Yale MFA graduate's painting is on this issue's cover.

INTERVIEW WITH MIDWEST BOOK REVIEW'S EDITOR, JIM COX ($15, 146PP, 6X9", ISBN: 978-1-546759-21-8): This issue includes an interview with Jim Cox, who has been editing the *Midwest Book Review* for over four decades, publishing thousands, if not hundreds of thousands of book reviews, with a focus on books from small presses that typically struggle with finding interested reviewers. Jim opens up about the realities of making a living from operating a review publication. His insight is essential to any author interested in self-promotion, and who is interested in how the review process looks from the other perspective. The "Introduction" features an aside from the Editor on the plague plagiarism is on American culture and society. The Editor also reviews dozens of new scholarly book releases. A critical essay by Swan Kim (Assistant Professor of English at Bronx Community College) analyzes Chinese female identity in Haling Nieh's *Mulberry and Peach*. E. L. Risden (Professor of English at St. Norbert College) contributed a unique blend of brisk stories and poetic interludes. Two of PLJ's returning poets are once again featured, Louis Gallo and Howard Winn (Professor of English at SUNY), as well as some other great poets, such as Kevin Casey, S. R. Graham, Daniel Nemo, Rikki Santer, and John Zedolik.

INTERVIEW WITH MARY JO PUTNEY: Volume VII, Issue 2: ($10, 6X9", 80pp, ISBN: 978-1-68114-196-1, 10 photographs, Summer 2015): Features an interview with Mary Jo Putney, a best-selling romance author. A ten-time finalist for the Romance Writers of America RITA, she won RITAs for Dancing on the Wind and The Rake and the Reformer and is on the RWA Honor Roll for bestselling authors. She has also been awarded two Romantic Times Career Achievement Awards, four NJRW Golden Leaf awards, and the Romance Writers of America Nora Roberts Lifetime Achievement Award. Also, an interview with an established poet and interim director of the Creative Writing Program at the University of Connecticut, Sean Frederick Forbes, interviewed by Rodrigo Rodriguez.

INTERVIEW WITH OTTO PENZLER, OWNER OF MANHATTAN'S MYSTERIOUS BOOKSHOP AND PRESS ($15: 130PP, 6X9", 978-1-981866-36-6): In these pages, you will find an interview with Otto Penzler, the Owner of Manhattan's Mysterious Bookshop and Mysterious Press. He has owned several other publishing businesses over the years, and has edited some of the most prestigious mystery anthologies. He talks about diverse topics from ebooks to the power of the Big Four publishers to marketing strategies and onto buying space for a bookstore.. Then, Kathleen Murphey's (associate professor of English at the Community College of Philadelphia) essay analyzes rape myths in modern fantasy fiction. These heavy speculations are followed by short stories from Alan Fleishman, Mark Howard, M. T. Ingoldby and Michael A. Livingston. The poetry section includes pieces from Gale Acuff, Keith Moul, Howard Winn (Professor of English at SUNY), and John Zedolik.

INTERVIEW WITH D.J. BUTLER, LAWYER AND SPECULATIVE WRITER ($15, 210PP, 6X9": 978-1-719439-52-7): This PLJ issue presents an interview with D.J. Butler, who has had a successful career in corporate law, and has published several fantasy and children's books with top presses. also carries over forty, detailed book reviews of fiction, scholarly, general interest and art books by the editor, Anna Faktorovich.

OTHER TITLES

Michael Connelly
A Reader's Guide
Stan Schatt
$15, 150pp, 2012, HC/PB
ISBN: 978-1-937536-27-5

What Time Are You?
Jeffry Atwood and
Charles A. Calio
$15, 106pp, 2012, HC/PB
ISBN: 978-1-937536-28-2

Baby Pepper
Michelle Chen
$15, 52pp, 2012, HC/PB
ISBN: 978-1-937536-04-6

A Communion of Saints
Terence Culleton
$15, 2011, 76pp, HC/PB
ISBN: 978-1-937536-05-3

Mt. Tam
Philip Shepard
$25, 286pp, 2014, HC/PB
ISBN: 978-1-937536-59-6

Walloomsac:
A Roman Fleuve
David Slavitt
$20, 176pp, 2014, PB/E
ISBN: 978-1-68114-026-1

Eyes of the Slain Woman
Benjamin Kwakye
$20, 2012
ISBN: 978-1-937536-20-6

Truths of the Heart
G. L. Rockey
$25, 2012, 332pp
ISBN: 978-1460983386

The Way Things Go:
And Other Poems
Lucas Carpenter
$15, 80pp, 2013, HC/PB
ISBN: 978-1-937536-42-8

Sky Sandwiches
John F. Buckley
$15, 98pp, 2012, HC/PB
ISBN: 978-1-937536-32-9

Nadia
Jack Lawrence Luzkow
$20, 270pp, 2012, HC/PB
ISBN: 978-1-937536-30-5

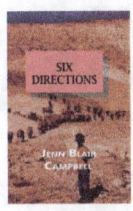

Six Directions
Jenn Blair Campbell
$15, 2011, 206pp, HC/PB
ISBN: 978-1-937536-03-9

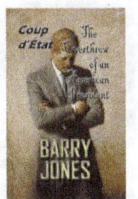

Coup d'Etat:
The Overthrow of an
American President
Barry Jones
$20, 126pp, 2014, HC/PB
ISBN: 978-1-937536-82-4

The Blue Maroon Murder
Gloria McMillan
$15, 202pp, 2011, HC/PB
ISBN: 978-1-937536-06-0

Rocks Full of Sky
Stephen Lefebure
$15, 88pp, 2013, HC/PB
ISBN: 978-1-937536-39-8

Rain, Rain, Go Away…
Mary Ann Hutchison:
$15, 132pp, 2011
ISBN: 978-1-937536-07-7

Ek-sen-trik-kuh Discordia
The Tales of Shamlicht
Reverend Loveshade
$15, 2011, 205pp, OOF
ISBN: 978-1-937536-18-3

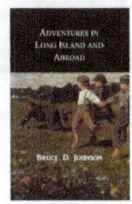

Adventures in Long
Island and Abroad
Bruce D. Johnson
$19.99, 2011, 348pp
ISBN: 978-1456549183

Under Centauri
Jeremy Gadd
$15, 96pp, 2013, HC/PB
ISBN: 978-1-937536-57-2

Class of '67: Fancies,
Myths and Follies
Paul Bellerive
$20, 148pp, HC/PB
ISBN: 978-1937536503

The Dandy Vigilante
Kevin Daley
$19, 252pp, 2014, HC/PB
ISBN: 978-1-937536-64-0

PLJ: Reviews of Popular
Fiction: Volume V:1
$10, 2013, 66pp
ISBN: 978-1-937536-46-6

PLJ: Volume V, Issue 3
Editor: Anna Faktorovich
$10, 2013, 160pp
ISBN: 978-1-937536-60-2

PLJ: Creative Work
Volume III: Issue 3
$10, Fall 2011, 68pp
ISBN: 978-1-937536-22-0

The Island of Charles
M. V. Montgomery
$15, 2013, 6X9", 98pp,
LCCN: 2013936553
ISBN: 978-1-937536-45-9

Romanticism
Catherine Corman
$15, 112pp, 6X9"
ISBN: 978-1-68114-213-5

The Code
Patricia Sweet
$15, 2014, 6X9", 126pp
ISBN: 978-1-937536-79-4

Meditation on Woman
Aline Soules
$15, 6X9", 80pp, 2011
ISBN: 978-1-937536-13-8

100 Years of the Fed
Marie Bussing-Burks
$15, 2011, 70pp
ISBN: 978-1-937536-17-6

Skewed
Philip Theibert
$20, 232pp, 2014
ISBN: 978-1-937536-95-4

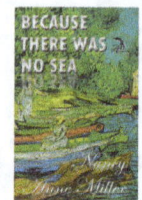

Because There Was No Sea
Nancy Anne Miller
$15, 86pp, 2014
ISBN: 978-1-937536-96-1

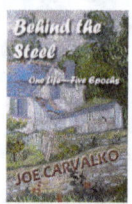

Behind the Steel
Joe Carvalko
$15/$30, 96pp, 2014
ISBN: 978-1-68114-005-6

*Poor Love
& Other Stories*
Anthony Labriola
$20, 174pp, 2014
ISBN: 978-1-68114-000-1

*The Pros and Cons of
Dragon-Slaying*
Anthony Labriola
$19, 338pp, 2014
ISBN: 978-1-937536-65-7

*Elvis Presley's Hips &
Mick Jagger's Lips*
Susana H. Case
$15, 80pp, 2013
ISBN: 978-1-937536-36-7

Earth and Below
Susana H. Case
$15, 112pp, 2013
ISBN: 978-1-937536-48-0

Skating in Concord
Jean LeBlanc
$15, 82pp, 2014
ISBN: 978-1-937536-80-0

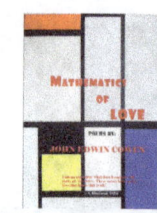

Mathematics of Love
John Edwin Cowen
$15, 134pp, 2011
ISBN: 978-1-937536-01-5

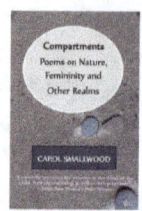

*Compartments: Poems on
Nature, Femininity...*
Carol Smallwood
$15, 146pp, 2011
ISBN: 978-1-937536-00-8

The Liver Bends in Time
Glen A. Mazis
$15, 110pp, 2012
ISBN: 978-1-937536-23-7

Devouring the Artist
Anthony Labriola
$15, 174pp, 2014
ISBN: 978-1-68114-165-7

Spirit of Tabasco
Richard Diedrichs
$15, 110pp, 2014
ISBN: 978-1-937536-89-3

*Dragonflies
in the Cowburbs*
Donelle Dreese
$15, 104pp, 2013
ISBN: 978-1-937536-51-0

The Sloths and I
Anna Faktorovich
$30, 32pp, 2013
ISBN: 978-1-937536-29-9

Inversed
Jason Holt
$15, 92pp, 2014
ISBN: 978-1-937536-62-6

Queen of the Platform
Laura Madeline Wiseman
$15, 84pp, 2013
ISBN: 978-1-937536-54-1

The Muscle Car Wars
B. J. Miller
$25, 396pp, 2015
ISBN: 978-1-68114-004-9

The Battle of Athens
Anna Faktorovich
$15, 56pp, 2012
ISBN: 978-1-937536-31-2

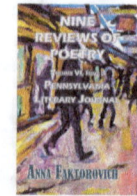

Nine Reviews of Poetry
Anna Faktorovich
$10, 148pp, 2014
ISBN: 978-1-68114-006-3

*British Literature
Volume 2, Issue 2*
$20, 2010, 208pp
ISBN: 978-1-456304-32-4

*New and Old Historical
Perspectives on
Literature: Vol. 2, Issue 1*
$15, 2010, 8.5X5.5", 272pp
ISBN: 978-1-450583-58-9

*PLJ: Editing Technique:
Vol. III, Issue 1*
**$10, 2011, 5.5X8.5", 114pp
ISBN: 978-1-461-16497-5**

*New Formalism of/on the
Contemporary: Vol. IV:1*
$10, 6X9", 144pp
ISBN: 978-1937536244

Silence Imbibed
Jenn Gutiérrez
$15, 2011, 100pp
ISBN: 978-1-937536107

East of Los Angeles
John Brantingham
$15, 72pp
ISBN#: 978-1460925201

Venom
S. K. Kelen
$15, 90pp
ISBN: 978-1456566418

*Crevices of Beautiful
Minds*
V. B. Kai-Rogers
$15/$30, 120pp, 2012
ISBN: 978-1-937536-31-2

*Private Hercules
McGraw: Poems of the
American Civil War*
S. Thomas Summers
$15/$30, 86pp, 2012
ISBN: 978-1-68114-172-5

*The Journal of Lt. Kendall
Everly: A Story of the
American Civil War*
S. Thomas Summers
$15/ $30, 80pp, 2013
978-1-68114-151-0

*Death Is Not the Worst
Thing*
T. Anders Carson
$15, 92pp, HC/PB
ISBN#: 978-1463518127

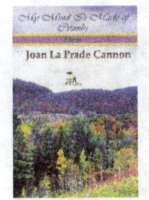
*My Mind Is Made of
Crumbs*
Joan La Prade Cannon
$15/$30, 100pp, 2013
ISBN: 978-1-68114-143-5

*Notes on the Road
to Now*
Paul Bellerive
$15/$30, 146pp, 2013
ISBN: 978-1-68114-150-3

Herculaneum's Fortune
Phylinda Moore
$15/$30, 78pp, 6X9", 2014
ISBN: 978-1-68114-134-3

Chanameed
Charles S. Kraszewski
$15, 124pp, 2014, HC/PB
IBSN: 978-1-503289-11-6

Liberation from Tyranny
Ronni Kove
$15/$30, 2014, 84pp
ISBN: 978-1-68114-128-2

*Folk Concert:
Changing Times*
Janet Ruth Heller
$15/$30, 90pp, 2012
ISBN: 978-1-68114-165-7

The Fool Returns
Tom Block
$20/$35, 250pp, 2014
ISBN: 978-1-68114-127-5

Third Law of Motion
Meg Files
$20/$35, 190pp, 2012
ISBN: 978-1-68114-169-5

Dancing in the Streets
Steven P. Unger
$20/$35, 208pp, 2012
ISBN: 978-1-68114-168-8

Blood Laws
Miguel Parga
$20/$35, 165pp, 2012
ISBN: 978-1-68114-161-9

Welcome Home, Sir
Steve Caplan
$15/$30, 154pp, 2011
ISBN: 978-1-68114-177-0

Eloquent Tattoo
Audrey Lavin
$15/$30, 162pp, 2012
ISBN: 978-1-68114-171-8

*The Private Side of a
Public Education*
Garry McGiboney
$15, 106pp, 2012, HC/PB
ISBN: 978-1-937536-19-0

*The Cross, or The
Chocolates that Exploded*
Vasyl Baziv
$20/$35, 248pp, 2013
ISBN: 978-1-68114-144-2

Bill Hope: His Story
Clifford Browder
$20/35, 2017, 158pp
ISBN: 978-1-68114-305-7

Up Against Beyond:
Selected Poems
Jason Holt
$20/35, 2010, 134pp
ISBN: 978-1-68114-317-0

The Cairo Arrangement:
A Novel
Bruce Colbert
$20/35, 2016, 6X9", 238pp
ISBN: 978-1-68114-284-5

An Adventurous Life:
Personal and Cultural
Robert Hauptman
$15/30, 142pp
ISBN: 978-1-937536-40-4

The Romances of
George Sand
Anna Faktorovich
$20/35, 2014, 252pp
ISBN: 978-1-937536-68-8

The Lonely Barber
Anthony Labriola
$20/35, 140pp, 2017
ISBN#: 978-1-68114-302-6

Clytemnestra's Last Day:
A Novel
S. Montana Katz
$20/35, 200pp, 2017
ISBN: 978-1-68114-329-3

Domestic Subversive: A
Feminist's Take
Roberta Salper
$20/35, 236pp, 2014
ISBN:978-1-937536-67-1

Radical Agrarian
Economics: Wendell Berry
Anna Faktorovich
$20/$35, 180pp, 2015
ISBN: 978-1-937536-91-6

Gender Bias in Mystery
and Romance Novel
Publishing: Mimicking
Anna Faktorovich
$20/ $35, 298pp, 2015
978-1-511888-90-5

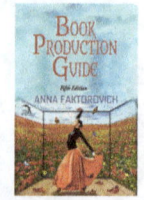

Book Production Guide
Anna Faktorovich
$10, 122pp, 2017 (5th Ed)
ISBN#: 978-1937536251

The Rig Veda:
First Mandala
David R. Slavitt
$20/35, 258pp, 7X10, 2015
ISBN: 978-1-68114-215-9

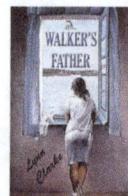

Walker's Father
Lynn Clarke
$20, 272pp, 2014
ISBN:978-1-68114-001-8

Evidence and Judgment
Lynn Clarke
$19.99, 244pp, 6X9", 2011
ISBN:978-1456501167

The Third of Seven
Jeremie Guy
$20/35, 274pp, 2016
ISBN: 978-1-68114-230-2

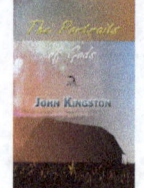

The Portraits of Gods
John Kingston
$20/35, 2015, 174pp
ISBN: 978-1-937536-88-6

The Battle against
Juvenile Bullying
Erin K. Leonard
$15/$30, 76pp, 2014
ISBN: 978-1-937536-99-2

Janet Yellen
Marie A. Bussing
$15/30, 48pp, 2015
ISBN: 978-1-68114-203-6

What Consumers Should
Know About Food Safety
David Walpuck
$15/30, 94pp, 2015
ISBN: 978-1-68114-221-0

How to See Beauty in
Life: Happier Living
North Wood
$15/30, 100pp, 2016
ISBN: 978-1-68114-205-0

Judas Was a Bishop: An
Old Man in His Church
William M. Shea
$20/$35, 330pp, 2015
ISBN: 978-1-68114-211-1

Where Gringos Don't
Belong
Robert Joe Stout
$20/35, 174pp
ISBN: 978-1-68114-123-7

Lombard Street: A Novel
Bruce Colbert
$20/35, 218pp, 2015
ISBN: 978-1-68114-185-5

Lessons for Leaders and
Governing Board
Garry McGiboney
$20/35, 240pp, 2014
ISBN: 978-1-937536-61-9

Friday: A Novel
Matthew R. K. Haynes
$15/30, 108pp, 2015
ISBN: 978-1-68114-105-3

Heroes' Tunnel
Christopher Grillo
$15/30, 2016, 6X9", 96pp,
LCCN: 2016935839
ISBN: 978-1-68114-253-1

Something Will Come to Us
Merrilee Cunningham
$15/30, 94pp, 2014
ISBN: 978-1-68114-129-9

Baudelaire's Revenge
Bob Van Laerhoven
$20/35, 2017
ISBN: 978-1-68114-310-1

Secrets of Gray Lake
Rebecca Duncan
$20/35, 190pp, 2015
ISBN: 978-1-68114-112-1

The Race Lost
Bruce Colbert
$15/30, 2015, 56pp
ISBN: 978-168114-194-7

Seven
Antonio J. Hopson
$15/30, 60pp, 2015
ISBN: 978-1-68114-096-4

Safari: Looking into the Eye of the Leopard
William J. Maloney
$20/35, 122pp, 2016
ISBN: 978-1-68114-293-7

When Leaves Change Color
John Bradford Branney
$19.90, 230pp, 2015
ISBN: 978-1-68114-191-6

The Uses of Money
William J. Palmer
$20/35, 188pp, 2016
ISBN: 978-1-68114-247-0

Architecture of Being: Selected Poems
Bruce Colbert
$15/30, 80pp, 2016
ISBN: 978-1-68114-259-3

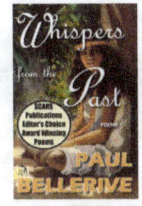
Whispers from the Past: Poems
Paul Bellerive
$15/30, 116pp, 2015
ISBN: 978-1-68114-189-3

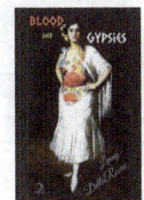
Blood and Gypsies
Lenny DellaRocca
$15/30, 78pp, 2016
ISBN: 978-1-68114-235-7

Medusa's Hairdresser: Skyclad
Maria Jacketti
$15/30, 94pp, 2015
ISBN: 978-1-68114-100-8

In Mercurial Days
Jim Berkheiser
$15/30, 104pp, 2015
ISBN: 978-1-68114-098-8

Handful of Sand and Other Poems
Steven P. Stamatis
$15/30, 92pp, 2015
ISBN: 978-1-68114-220-3

Disciplined Subjects and Better Selves: Essays
Omar Sabbagh
$20/35, 246pp, 2016
ISBN: 978-1-68114-290-6

Taino Sunrise: An Odyssey
Victor Rodriguez
$25/40, 456pp, 2016
ISBN: 978-1-68114-287-6

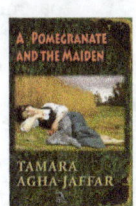
A Pomegranate and the Maiden
Tamara Agha-Jaffar
$20/35, 198pp, 2015
ISBN: 978-1-68114-209-8

Who Is Olivia Green?
David Heaton
$20/35, 202pp, 2015
ISBN: 978-1-68114-225-8

Revolution Time
Paul G. Varnas
$20/35, 242pp, 2016
ISBN: 978-1-68114-232-6

Armageddon at Maidan
Vasyl Baziv
$20/35, 166pp, 2016
ISBN: 978-1-68114-227-2

Invisible Mending: Poems
Anthony Labriola
$20, 134pp, 2015
ISBN: 978-1-68114-009-4

Film Theory and Modern Art
Anna Faktorovich
$10, , Spring 2014, 136pp
ISBN: 978-1-937536-72-5

The Blessing of the Bikes & Other Life-Cycles
Anthony Labriola
$15, 112pp, 2016
ISBN: 978-1-937536-35-0

The Intersection Between Dance and Art
Anna Faktorovich
$20, color, 96pp, 2016
ISBN: 978-1-541227-40-8

ORDER FORM

All books in this catalog are available through **Ingram, YBP, Coutts Information Services, EBSCO, TotalBooX, ProQuest, Follett, Barnes and Noble, Amazon** and various other distribution channels. A variety of distributors are available to meet the needs of the majority of book buyers. Buyers can also order directly from Anaphora if they need 5 or more books to be shipped to a single location. Note: Hardcover editions are available for all books in the catalog, but some of them are only available in short run prints directly from Anaphora (as the hardcovers are only distributed through Ingram for 1 year after release). Soft cover books remain in print indefinitely.

To make a purchase: e-mail the amount of books you need, the address where they should go, your preferred payment method (PayPal, SquareUp, check, bank electronic transfer) and preferred discount percentage (40-55%). If you buy titles from Ingram, they come with a 40% distribution discount. Book shipments and printing speeds can be expedited at an extra cost, so please specify if you need the books in less than 2-3 weeks. Standard shipping for 5+ books is included in the price when shipping to US, UK, AU and CA. Shipping to other countries can take 6+ weeks and has varying costs.

Returns: Some of the books are refundable (check with Anaphora for details on specific titles). Most books are not returnable because books have to be destroyed and cannot be resold after a return. You can ask for the books you buy to be returnable, and for this the author would have to agree to take on any resulting losses.

For Reviewers: e-mail Anaphora for free PDF or printed review copies of any books in this Catalog.

Mail or e-mail Orders To
(address is subject to change):
Anaphora Literary Press
Anna Faktorovich, Ph.D.
1108 W 3rd Street
Quanah, TX 79252

Contact With Questions/ Orders:
director@anaphoraliterary.com
1-470-289-6395 (12pm-9pm CST Mon-Sun)

ISBN 13: 978-1-68114-479-5
ISBN 10: 1-68114-479-4

QUANTITY	TITLE	COST
	SUBTOTAL	
Distribution Discount for orders of 5+ books: 40-55% depending on preference		
Shipping to US/UK/AU/CA for 5+ included Ask for shipping rates to other countries		
Expedited shipping and printing rates available upon request		
Optional Donation		
	TOTAL	

Checks, electronic banking transfers, SquareUp, and PayPal payments are accepted. Please fill out the information below and send the check to the address on the side bar. There is an extra 4/3% charge to use PayPal/SquareUp: e-mail for instructions.

Name: _____

Address: _____

City: _____ State: _____ Code: _____

Telephone: _____

E-Mail: _____

www.ingramcontent.com/pod-product-compliance
Lightning Source LLC
Chambersburg PA
CBHW080811120626
46556CB00009B/3294